Competing for Capital—A Financial Relations Approach
Bruce W. Marcus

How to Improve Profitability through More Effective Planning
Thomas S. Dudick

Financial Analysis and Business Decisions on the Pocket Calculator
Jon M. Smith

Managing Innovation
Edwin A. Gee and Chaplin Tyler

The Management System: Systems Are for People
Leslie H. Matthies

The Management System

About the Author

LESLIE H. MATTHIES received his B.S. from the University of California, Berkeley in 1933. For over 30 years, he has worked in systems applications and applied systems education. Referred to as the "dean of systems", Matthies founded the Systemation Company and managed it for over 12 years. In 1971 he turned over the management to new owners. He is now associated with the not-for-profit Management Research Society, which he also founded in 1974.

His educational writings include articles and books on management and systems, and courses in professional systems, basic systems, and forms design. He is an internationally known speaker, seminar leader, and developer of workshops in clear systems writing, introduction to project management, and essentials of systems analysis.

In 1958, the Systems and Procedures Association (now the Association for Systems Management) presented Matthies with the System-Man-of-the-Year Award. In addition to directing systems departments in large corporations, he has aided many smaller companies as a consultant and as a member of the board of directors.

The Management System

Systems Are for People

LESLIE H. MATTHIES

Management Research Society

A Wiley-Interscience Publication

JOHN WILEY & SONS New York · London · Sydney · Toronto

Library of Congress Cataloging in Publication Data

Matthies, Leslie H.
   The management system.

   (Wiley series on systems and controls for financial management)
   "A Wiley-Interscience publication."
   Includes index.
   1. System analysis.   2. Management.   I. Title.

HD20.5.M378   658.4'032   76-4572
ISBN 0-471-57697-2

Printed in the United States of America

10 9 8 7 6 5 4 3 2 1

To the memory of the pioneers of scientific management, particularly Frank and Lillian Gilbreth, Mary Parker Follett, Henri Fayol, and Frederick W. Taylor

FOREWORD

Many years ago, I had occasion to design my first system and write my first procedure. The procedure literally had everything—policy, editorials, commandments, humor, and, surprisingly, a little of what should have been in it . . . a procedure. It was twenty-seven pages long when finished! That was about twenty years ago. Although many of the points it covered are still valid, I'll bet that, to this date, I'm the only person who has ever read it completely.

That was before I met Les Matthies, the author of this book.

All too few of us find ourselves in the right place at the right time, in a position where we are privileged to make a seminal contribtuion to our chosen profession. Mr. Matthies is one of the lucky ones. More importantly, however, he recognized his opportunity and he took advantage of it. As a result, all of us who have labored in the systems vineyard and all of us who have worked with those who have so labored, have been his beneficiaries.

As with any new discipline, but particularly one that has developed so rapidly, the systems field is replete with earnest but misguided souls who contribute to the noise and fury surrounding systems, but little to its advance; with some outright charlatans, who contribute to management's disenchantment with systems; and with missionaries who proselytize systems . . . especially the hardware . . . but rarely with a favorable impact on the bottom line.

Again, as with any new discipline, systems has had all too few individuals whose contributcons to their chosen field can truly be called "basic." Mr. Matthies richly deserves his title, the "Dean of Systems." His contributions have been numerous and varied. Whether we are aware of it or not, all of us in systems and all of us in management have been affected by them. His "four star" rules of good writing, his "Playscript" procedure-writing technique, his emphasis on data and data analysis, his concept of the form as a carrier of data . . . to name just a few . . . have made life easier for all of us.

But I like to think that his finest contribution to the systems field has been his continued emphasis on the basics of systems. Time after time, Les has brought young systems people, who have become enamored of the latest shiny hardware, or the newest technical language, or the most elegant new programs, back to the realization that their job is to develop systems that will serve management. Any of us in management recognize what a crying need there is for a continued reiteration of this point. How often we are part of those frustrating dialogues between management on one hand and the systems analyst-programmer-technician on the other. Neither knows nor appreciates what the other is trying to say. The communications gap seems as wide as ever. How often must we cry: "Management's needs come first! Does the system do the job management wants done?"

It is a distinct privilege, therefore, to introduce this book in which the author tells the how, the what, and the why of "The Management System." The emphasis on "management" is properly placed.

Management has the need; management also has the responsibility. Yet, in systems at least, management rarely has the know-how. And even more rarely does the system technician have the management concept of a system. In this book, the author has distilled the essentials of the "Management System" from a lifetime of experience in systems work . . . as a practitioner, as an author, as a teacher, but primarily as a creative thinker and contributor.

Those many thousands of you who have met Les in person or through his voluminous writings will find in this volume a refreshing reacquaintance with this stimulating individual whose ideas are ever new, ever expanding, and ever eminently practical. Those of you, whether in management, or in finance, or in the systems field, who have never met the author are in for a rare treat. You'll find his ideas and the way he presents them deceptively simple, but absolutely essential to a full understanding of that vital concept of the modern business-world—the "management system."

ROBERT L. SHULTIS

SERIES PREFACE

No one needs to tell the reader that the world is changing. He sees it all too clearly. The immutable, the constant, the unchanging of a decade or two ago no longer represent the latest thinking—on *any* subject, whether morals, medicine, politics, economics, or religion. Change has always been with us, but the pace has been accelerating, especially in the postwar years.

Business, particularly with the advent of the electronic computer some 20 years ago, has also undergone change. New disciplines have sprung up. New professions are born. New skills are in demand. And the need is ever greater to blend the new skills with those of the older professions to meet the demands of modern business.

The accounting and financial functions certainly are no exception. The constancy of change is as pervasive in these fields as it is in any other. Industry is moving toward an integration of many of the information gathering, processing, and analyzing functions under the impetus of the so-called systems approach. Such corporate territory has been, traditionally, the responsibility of the accountant and the financial man. It still is, to a large extent—but times are changing.

Does this, then, spell the early demise of the accountant as we know him today? Does it augur a lessening of influence for the financial specialists in today's corporate hierarchy? We think not. We maintain, however, that it is incumbent upon today's accountant and today's financial man to learn *today's* thinking and to *use today's* skills. It is for this reason the Wiley Series on Systems and Controls for Financial Management is being developed.

Recognizing the broad spectrum of interests and activities that the series title encompasses, we plan a number of volumes, each representing the latest thinking, written by a recognized authority, on a particular facet of the financial man's responsibilities. The subjects contemplated for discussion within the series range from production accounting systems to planning, to corporate records, to control of cash. Each book is an in-depth study of one subject within this group. Each is intended to be a practical, working tool for the businessman in general and the financial man and accountant in particular.

ROBERT L. SHULTIS
FRANK M. MASTROMANO

PREFACE

The term "management" has two meanings: (1) a *group of people* who direct the activities of other people and (2) a *process* that all people use to get their organization's work done.

In this book we give our attention to the second meaning . . . to the process called a *management* system. The term "system" has many meanings. However we confine our attention to just one type of system—the *management system*.

In every organization the management process operates on data . . . information used by executives, managers, supervisors, workers, staff people. These people act on or they react to data. Work goes on or stops or changes, depending on the data that reaches people.

Each person in the organization needs specific information to be able to carry on his or her work. To start our consideration of the management system and how to improve it, let us ask three questions:

1. Does anyone know exactly what information each man and each woman in the organization needs to carry on work?
2. How much of the effort now expended on computerization makes a direct contribution to essential systems actions? And, conversely, how much work in the computer room is necessary just because you're using a computer?
3. If you can examine a system, how can you judge whether it is a poor system or a good one?

Give some thought to each of those questions. Some people don't know the answers. Do you?

When systems improvement work began to emerge as a distinct, identifiable type of staff activity, people thought of it as being confined to the office or to the accounting area.

Now we know better. Major management systems thread through every activity in the organization . . . through purchasing, selling, production, design-ing, and transportation. The various systems in the organization provide work links among the many people who do specialized work. The total of a selected gathering of individual work efforts is a coordinated whole that we call the sys-tem.

Thus the person doing systems analysis work must consider all activity aspects of the organization . . . from sales through shipping, from engineering through production, from claim through settlement. People are doing systems analysis in all types of organizations . . . insurance companies, banks, govern-ment agencies, military institutions, industries, utilities, churches, labor un-ions. Most of this analysis work presupposes that the resulting system will be run on the computer.

What is the relationship between the system and the people who make up the management group? This relationship was well expressed by Colonel Lyndall Urwick, British international consultant:

Today an organization is essentially a complicated system of cooperation—in itself a single machine—in which effectiveness is dependent less and less on the quality of indi-vidual effort—and more and more on the logic of the total design—and upon the precision with which each individual's contribution is geared to the overall plan.

The system is the only device that we could use to "precisely gear each indi-vidual's contribution to the overall plan."

People tend to think of the terms *systems* and *computers* as synonyms. The two are not the same. But just how do systems and computers relate to each other? Can you design a good system and not use a computer? Can a poor sys-tem run on a computer?

We owe a debt to the computer. It made us *think!* What is data? What is a system? What is a method? What is paperwork?

At this point let's clarify our use of the term *data*. We recognize that people in the academic world still say "data are" and "datum is." Not so in the practicing world of systems. Here data, like sheep, is both singular and plural. Whoever heard of "processing a datum?"

The computer brought definition and focus to the phenomenon known as "paperwork." Before the advent of the computer people thought of data pro-cessing as just clerical work or bookkeeping or "paperwork." Most data pro-cessing took place in one department . . . accounting.

Yet a study made in an aircraft factory during World War II indicated that only 7% of the total amount of paper and forms in use were generated by the accounting department: 93% of it was used elsewhere!

Almost every large organization today (at least in Canada and the United

States) uses one or more computers. Now it's the turn of the smaller organization. Here come the minicomputers such as Basic-Four's 350, DEC's DPD-11, or IBM's system/32. Probably 350,000 organizations that did not use a computer in 1976 will be using one in 1980. This brings up an important question:

> Will the executives of the new computer users make the same mistake that their "big brother" executives made in their big organizations in the 1960's? The mistake? Computerizing *before* they systematized.

Can these smaller organizations afford financial bloopers? In the past a few companies have even gone into bankruptcy because of such errors. Others have been staggered by a severe drain on their capital resources. None of that was necessary. We can say this to any chief executive officer:

> Go into any automation program only when you know your *systems-eyes* are wide open!

Do that. Then the marvelous equipment that surrounds the computer can serve you well. As a matter of fact, *great* systems, not just good systems, can be yours.

You see, the quality of a system is not primarily dependent on a computer's hardware, software, or programs. The quality of a system depends on two essential factors: (1) on the *design* of that system and (2) on how much the users of that system *participated* in the development. Systems designed entirely by professional analysts have two characteristics: processing efficiency and sterility. Another name? Cold fish system.

Above all else this book stresses participation in systems design. That is what this book is about—the design of a true *management* system . . . a joint product of a systems designer and a systems user.

When the design of each system is exactly right for the organization and for that specific application . . . the marvelous data processing machine facilities can be moved in to make their contributions to the doing of business. Our aim may as well be high. So let's make it this:

> A network of great systems throughout the organization!

LESLIE H. MATTHIES

Colorado Springs, Colorado
June 1976

CONTENTS

provide for the three systems functions . . . make reports a part of your systems plan . . . your creativity peak . . . bring all the ideas in focus . . . develop a title for the system . . . coordination is next . . . expert opinions . . . wrap it up

Four interested groups of people . . . what do the operating people think? . . . make all elements visible . . . don't tell all . . . give your new system a lively title . . . executive approval . . . executive interests are different . . . written or spoken? . . . benefits and losses: words that move men . . . the physical form of the proposal . . . presentation at a meeting . . . typical timing . . . don't be wishy-washy . . . ask for the order . . . what to do with a rejection?

You install it: don't drop the ball now . . . project work is different . . . dangers in project handling . . . new in: old out. when? . . . break down the installation job . . . time and money . . . types of time . . . who estimates the time and money needed? . . . put the subjobs in sequence . . . develop individual specification sheets . . . Gantt chart: picture of the project . . . be people conscious . . . show concern for the people . . . skills and training . . . walk the cycle beat . . . that learning curve.

Four marks of a management system . . . honeymoon with the computer . . . the contribution principle . . . other wonderful work the computer does . . . divide the work again . . . what management systems are most used? . . . concentrate on inputs and outputs . . . the computer is for the user's use . . . the computer is "file oriented" . . . the four members of the computer's "immediate family" . . . running a pay system with the superclerk . . . programming languages . . . inventory: everybody's system . . . decision aids . . . computer-generated reports . . . computer action on an inventory . . . what work needs to be done? . . . work caused because you use the computer . . . the scale of business

The Management System

THE MANAGEMENT PROCESS

Every member of an organization has a "management" responsibility. The secretary has hers, the truck driver has his, the police officer has his. The job is that of managing *work*. By managing his work each man (or each woman) gets a result. The sum total of each person's work gets results for the organization.

1. PEOPLE GET RESULTS

Results? What results? Why, things like selling goods or services . . . manufacturing articles . . . shipping goods . . . collecting money . . . paying out money . . . inventing new products . . . revising and updating old products.

Consider the job of shipping goods. One man may do the crating, another man the weighing, while a woman prepares bills of lading. A clerk may schedule the pickups, answer phone inquiries, or notify the billing operator to write the invoices.

Each man and each woman manages work: each does a portion of the total job of shipping.

If each individual manages to do his portion of work well, is that enough to guarantee results for the organization? No. Not quite. Each job must be managed in coordination with each *related* job.

How do you increase your *organization's* effectiveness if, as Colonel Urwick states (see Preface), it is dependent on the precision with which each individual's contribution is geared to the overall plan?

Can one person, perhaps a systems analyst, do this job Urwick refers to as

1

"precision gearing"? Can a manager do it? A supervisor? A consultant? A computer expert? A chief executive officer?

All people in your organization may not be eligible to join the management club, but all people shoulder some management responsibility. They must play a role in the management *process*.

So we are interested in management as a process, not primarily as a separate group of people.

2. THE PROCESS OF MANAGING

Again let's ask, "What is management?" We first think of it as a group of people (managers and supervisors) who see that other people get work done. But management is also a process of managing the organization's business.

In that light, everyone has a management responsibility and takes part in the process. It is just that supervisors and managers have specific and unique roles . . . but so do the operators . . . and so do the top-level executives.

These unique roles in the process can be defined somewhat as follows:

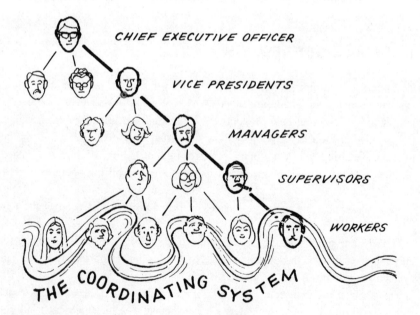

The system is the coordinating element of management, getting results at the working level.

1. *An operator* does one specific type of job, involving one or more tasks. He works under the supervision of someone else. When he masters his job, he takes a management role. He possesses a working skill and he applies it, along with this attitude: "This specific result is my responsibility; I'll manage it as I work."
2. *Clerks* and their machines (including the computer) are scorekeepers and data processors.
3. *A supervisor* directly oversees the work of a group of operators.
4. *A manager* directs the work of a group of supervisors.
5. *A general manager* directs the work of managers.
6. *A vice-president* is in charge of one major, specialized work segment of the organization's total work. As such he directs the work of general managers within that work specialty segment.

Organization structure alone is static. It comes to life when the people communicate through the system.

7. *A chief executive officer* coordinates, at the top, the work of all the organization's specialized work segments.
8. *The system* is the device used in the management process to coordinate, at the working level, all the contributions provided by the many work specialists.

All the seven categories of people listed are systems *users*. They all need information so they can do the job assigned to them.

OK. There are some roles that some people play. There are other roles, too. Now what hangs the everyday human drama together? What makes the organization structure come alive and throb with activity? Conventionally we think:

Well, that's easy to answer. The people who are assigned supervisory or management roles give orders to the people who work for them. The chief executive officer makes known what he wants done to the vice-president, who tells the general manager, who passes it on to the supervisor (by way of the manager), and when the operator finally gets the word, he goes to work. As everybody knows, that's the way you activate the organizational structure.

Simple enough. A boss decides what work is to be done. Then he tells his workers to do it and they do it. That's the process:

Decision . . . order . . . execution . . . work done . . . results obtained.

This is a lingering vision. Possibly it was true of the managing process 100 years ago. It isn't true today.

If you are a boss (or have been one), you know that you did not get work done through people by giving orders all day long. Very likely you didn't give anyone one order a week. But the work went on, didn't it? You might have explained it this way:

We reduced the work to a routine, trained each worker, and then each person did his job. If there was a hitch somewhere, like a bottleneck, I moved in and straightened it out.

Exactly. Do you know what you just said? "We reduced the work to be done to a routine and then each person did his job." You almost described a system, even if you didn't call it that.

3. DATA NEEDS ARE NOT MET

To carry on work, each person needs a specific selection of information. The order clerk needs a particular set of data that is not the same as the set of data the shipping clerk needs.

The general manager needs information that helps him to carry out his responsibilities. His data set is not the same as the supervisor's. To do his work, the accountant needs a set of information that is quite unlike the set the truck driver uses.

Some work specialists, such as auditors, need large amounts of information. Other work specialists, such as janitors or security guards, need much smaller amounts. If the person gets just the right kind of information, and it is available when he needs it, each man can carry on (manage) his portion of the management process.

A judicious supply of the required information to each member of the work team is the mark not only of a good system, but of a *great* system.

But what do people get out of the average, mediocre system? Floods of information, most of it not usable. Some information is redundant . . . and useless. One supervisor said, "The data processing people tell me what I told them 30 days before."

High-speed printers roll out zigzag packs of "activity recitals", sometimes at the rate of 2000 lines per minute! As one user put it: "They just let the computer spill its guts on paper and send me enough paper each week to fill a file drawer. Do I read it? Don't be funny. It would take me 50 or 60 hours a week. And even then it would mean nothing. Full of codes."

The danger of such blind data-spewing practices is that buried under the avalanche of useless data may be some vital information that the user should read.

Look at the data display on the average on-line terminal. Is it arranged so that it is really meaningful to the viewer? Or is the display arranged for the convenience of the central processing unit, so that the data can come out arranged just as they are stored in the computer's high-speed memory?

Why does such a situation exist? Simply because the systems *user* and the systems *designer* have not worked together. So the designer, feeling that something must come out of the computer, arranges to spew out reports because years before somebody spewed them out before in a previous system that also failed to serve the user.

Often the user ignores the stacks of computer-produced paper. He jury-rigs his own reporting system with the help of a clerk. There are some exceptions to these situations. They are the ones that make the news.

The systems analyst knows what his equipment needs, but he often does not know what the systems user needs. Sometimes he doesn't know what business his organization really is in. He thinks it is in the data processing business.

The entire management process must be served. And it will only be served when user and analyst, working together, find the answer to this question for each man and each woman:

What data do I need to carry on my portion of the total management process? How much of it can the system supply?

4. THE TECHNICAL WHIRLWIND

Let us understand the problems of the computer analyst and the computer programmer. These professional people have been working in a technical whirlwind for more than 15 years. It is still whirling.

These data processing men and women hardly become acquainted with one set of techniques before another wave of developments rolls over them. They not only have the computer to deal with but they have the storage areas, diskettes, disks, floppy disks, tapes, and even microfilm/computer interfaces (COM). They must delve into the complexity of the computer and consider all its supporting gear, including card-readers, printers and sorters. In the last few years, a series of telecommunication networks . . . wire or microwave connections between computers and their related terminals . . . and sometimes between computers and computers . . . have appeared, adding to the complexity.

The analysts and programmers learn structured programming, new "languages" . . . they learn about the technique of virtual storage, partitioning high-speed memory, operating programs, multiprocessing, on-line and batch processing techniques, just to name a few.

Most of these people who are working to master the technical intricacies of the computer world are dedicated professionals. They devote considerable skills and energies to make the systems installations work on the machines. The point is this: Because they have been forced to cope with one technical development after another, there is a communication gap between systems users and systems designers. We can't blame anyone, neither user nor technical person. But the gap is there. Users and designers aren't talking to each other, and that cannot go on.

Now our effort, our energy, and our attention must be concentrated on the job of changing the situation. We can do it. We can close the communication gap to the extent that the computer people and the users of systems will work together on a friendly, cooperative basis.

And when that happens, properly functioning systems of the organization will permit the expansion of the systems analysis field! Not only will we have top-grade big systems . . . we will also have numerous top-grade smaller systems.

CHAPTER 2

WHAT IS A MANAGEMENT SYSTEM?

If you ask the average man, "What is a system?" the chances are that he will reply, "It's a computer."

Actually we are surrounded by all types of systems . . . electrical, air transport, hydraulic, truck transportation, school, railroad, gas transmission, library, fuel (for engines), and river systems. Each is truly a system. The term itself conveys the meaning of something that is a whole but is made up of many parts, components,* or subsystems. Even a subsystem can have subsubsystems. Within an auto, the fuel system is a whole, but it is made up of individual components such as the carburetor, the fuel pump, the gas lines, the fuel gauge, and the storage tank.

The word *system* is a popular buzz word. Business men use it to help sell equipment, supplies, or the services of skilled people. People who sell computers, computer software, printed forms, copy machines, duplicators, or microfilm equipment . . . all have used the term *system* in connection with their products.

In this book we consider only one type of system . . . the *management* system. Like other systems, the management system carries a meaning of a wholeness. In common with other systems, it too is composed of a number of parts or subsystems.

---

* Components = parts of something whole; constituent ingredients.

Let's focus on one type of system: a management system.

1. TYPICAL SYSTEMS APPLICATIONS

In an organization you can classify the total routine work into such activities as:

Making sales to customers
Paying employees
Paying vendors
"Keeping time" of the working employees
Updating the inventory records
Billing customers
Producing articles
Inspecting and checking articles
Requesting articles or items (from the stock room)
Making claims
Delivering
Receiving
Procuring goods and materials

Each activity is coupled with a related system. Thus the work of paying employees is a *payroll system*. The work of paying vendors uses a system called *accounts payable*, an accounting term. The activity of procurement is a system called *purchasing*.

Consider the sequence of activities in a purchasing system. The action starts when a person in the stock room discovers the need for a new supply of an item. He requests the item by filling out a paper form (a requisition) and then he gets his boss's approval. Next he sends the requisition to the purchasing department, where a clerk gives it to the buyer who buys the item.

The buyer selects a supplier (vendor) and then fills out a purchase order. After the purchasing agent (or the chief buyer) approves the purchase order, the clerk mails it to the supplier, and the process continues.

2. COMPLEXITY IS THE ENEMY OF UNDERSTANDING

A director of management information services told a group of working supervisors how and why their organization changed computer equipment. He said:

The software enabled us to move our DOS/VS workload directly to the new equipment. We attached our full speed 3333-equivalent 7733 disk drives, thus providing higher speed secondary storage. The new equipment is configured with 256K bytes of core. We reduced the time to run jobs without changing core allocations and expect to improve core availability by more effective I/O blocking.

The supervisors shook their heads. They didn't know what the data processing man meant.

That statement might make sense to another technician, but to a systems user it is a complex form of jargon . . . even gibberish.

Now when a "director of management information services" talks to supervisors, does the firm also need a director of plain English information for interpreting what the first director has said?

Such a communication failure is a pity. The *real* objective of each system is so simple . . . to buy . . . to sell . . . to pay . . . to collect . . . to ship . . . to design . . . . to supply . . . to receive.

The technical manager of data processing tends to immerse himself in the complexities of his technology, which does in fact require considerable "coping with." So he has little time to listen to the user or even try to communicate with him. When you use the computer as a focal point for running any system, you *create* problems and challenges. Probably 50% of your computer problems exist because you use the computer.

As far as the real value of the system is concerned, in the area of getting results, many aspects of the computer complex are nonproductive.

Let's not get smothered in technical complexity. We can view the system as a "pure management system." We will *not* assume that we are going to draw on the resources that a computer could provide. Maybe we'll use one. Maybe we won't.

Don't misunderstand. We do not advise people not to use the computer. Not at all. The scale on which we do business today would be impossible without the aid of the computer. A top executive of the Bank of America expressed it something like this:

> If we didn't use computers today, we'd need to use the services of every adult in California to do our account keeping for us.

The general, sensible approach is this: design your system to get the required result with the least work effort. Then turn around and ask, "Who can do the work required to process the transaction . . . to move it along and complete it?" Only then does it make sense to select the system's requirements . . . the people, the machines, the equipment, or any outside services. You should not ask: "What computer should we select?" You should ask: "What work needs to be done? Can a computer do some of that work? Can it do it better than a person can?" Only if the answer is "yes" to the question of computer usage do you ask *which* machines you should use.

Let's avoid complexity and technical details. If we do, we can turn our attention to an activity you probably never saw *as a system*. So let's ask again: "What is a system?" We can look for answers by observing four different systems in action.

Our first system is so deceptively simple that you may never have suspected that it is a system. But it is.

3. A CAFE'S ORDER PROCESSING SYSTEM

A woman enters a small cafe and says to the waitress: "One hamburger to go with everything but onions."

The waitress writes the order on her cafe checkpad, then relays the order to the cook, saying: "One burger to go. Hold the onion. Everything else."

To ensure accuracy in the data transmission process, the cook repeats the order: "One burger to go with everything. Hold the onions."

In this bit of action, we can see the simple data flow of a "short cycle" system. To fulfill her human need for something to eat, the customer started the

action (triggered the transaction) by ordering a hamburger.

Notice how the data passed from one person to another. The waitress relays (orally) the customer's order to the production man (the cook), who prepares the hamburger, then passes it to the waitress. She wraps it, tells the customer the price, collects the money, opens the cash drawer, rings up the sale, places the meal check in the cash drawer, and gives the hamburger and change to the customer, who then leaves with her purchase.

Here the systems cycle (or total sequence of steps) is short. It is so short that the customer, the waitress, and the cook use spoken orders. But data was passed from one person to another. Although not in written form, the orders were still data. The only written data used appeared on the printed form (the cafe checkpad).

Observation: The customer pulled the action "trigger." She came into the cafe to satisfy a need . . . her hunger. The waitress and the cook, each operators with specific types of work to do, worked as a team and fulfilled that customer's need. The cycle was complete when the customer paid and walked out the door with her hamburger.

The action in this scene took place quickly, yet you can identify five very short, but distinct systems cycles, each linked to the next in a fast-moving sequence:

1. A sales (ordering) system
2. A production system
3. A delivery system
4. A billing system
5. A money collection system

In this systems sequence only the action aspects are visible. It's likely that the other aspects, such as management control, also exist. It is likely that the cafe owner (absent at the moment) can check the balance between the incoming food materials (raw materials) and the outgoing, finished goods (the cooked hamburger).

Observe these characteristics in the cafe system example:

1. Three different actors took part.
2. Action resulted from the passing of data from one person to another.
3. You could see the *start* of the systems cycle and its *end*. The transaction started when the customer placed her order. It ended when she walked out with the hamburger.
4. The system enabled two people, the cook and the waitress, to do different types of work and at the same time to work as a team. Their respective contributions were different, but they were coordinated.

4. A PRODUCTION SYSTEM IN A SMALL MACHINE SHOP

Our next example of a system includes more complex factors. Here we can observe an important systems factor—management control.

In the following action, only three characters appear: (1) the customer, (2) the owner-salesman, and (3) the machine operator.

In the first scene the owner-salesman is in the office of his customer, the Forin Manufacturing Company. Mr. Forin is signing an order for flexible couplings. The customer not only needs these couplings, he needs them in 12 days. Meeting delivery promises to *his* customers depends on the delivery service that he gets from suppliers.

The owner-salesman promises, "We'll make it." Here we identify the start of a transaction . . . the trigger.

In scene two, it is 8 a.m. The owner-salesman is giving the action form (SALES ORDER) to one of his machine operators. This is the data hand-off: one person passed data on to the next actor in the channel. In a systems channel frequently one actor passes action-getting information on to the next actor.

While the key data that the operator will need are on the order, the operator is receiving additional information from his boss as, "Start work on them today." But also notice an envelope hanging on the operator's machine labeled JOB SPECS. Detailed information related to the manufacture of flexible couplings is in "storage" there (a systems memory).

Undoubtedly the SALES ORDER, or a copy of it, also serves as a requisition on the stockroom. The operator acknowledges receipt of his orders by saying, "I'll get the castings."

5.   AUTHORITY TO USE TIME
AND MATERIALS

By handing the operator the SALES ORDER, the owner-salesman has authorized the worker to work on a specific job. By passing action information on to the worker, he has authorized him to use his working *time* on that order. The

worker's time is of value, one of the resources that a manager uses to get results. And of course the time not only creates value through the worker's efforts, but the worker must be paid; thus there is always a cost in the use of time.

Observation: People in an organization cannot use their time in any way they choose, or for personal activities. They use it in response to data provided by the system. In our example the owner-salesman is serving as a link in the action sequence. In larger operations, an order processing clerk or planning supervisor would perform that function.

Time is one valuable resource. Another is material. So in our next scene the worker is carrying a box of castings that he will use to produce (fabricate) the flexible couplings. Notice the part number: 48692. This is "key information" and subsequent inventory action will pivot around that number.

In the next scene (the fourth) it is 8:06 a.m. and the worker has laid out all the information needed to do the job. Apparently flexible couplings (part 48962) are not articles the operator makes often. So he uses other documents to refresh his memory. These have been stored in a transparent envelope labeled JOB SPECS. This array of information includes a job outline, routing, time

❸ MATERIAL

❹ DATA AT WORK STATION

standards, and detailed specifications that relate to part 48962. Included of course is the action form itself, the SALES ORDER.

Observation: So far we've seen characteristics of a system that are universal. The action form carries authority to take work action, thus to use time. It also authorizes the use of other resources such as materials. A regular shop order used in a production system also fulfills this function. So does a sales order . . . and so does a requisition on the stock room.

The common denominator of time usage and of material usage is, of course, money.

In this example the total time needed to complete the order will be 10 working days. OK. The worker has been at work all day. It is now near the end of the first day. The operator has been machining the couplings. *Question:* Since the owner-salesman is not present, how does he know the worker is putting in a fair day's work on these articles? The owner can't be looking over the machine operator's shoulder. He has other things to do. How does he exercise control over the work action?

Some people think it is sufficient to release an order that calls for action by dropping it into the "systems channel." But that isn't enough in a real management system. The system must give a manager some way to exercise manage-

ment *control* over action. Let's see how our ownersalesman does this.

As the machinist works during the day, he places each finished coupling in one of two boxes. One box is labeled GOOD PARTS, the other is labeled REJECTS.

Observation: Consider the systems principle behind this separation of the parts into the two boxes. The principle is this: The first purpose of the system is to get work action. This is accomplished by providing data to people (or machines) permitting them to react to that data and take the required action. The supplemental purpose is control. But if a manager is to control, he can't wait for the completion of the action (10 days). He must be assured that the action *is* taking place and *is* in accordance with his planning for it. This planning is probably reflected in the time and quality standards for part 48692.

With his knowledge of what *should* be, the man in management is in a position to control the action. This is an essential feature of a management system.

But to supply feedback, or knowledge of actual results, the system must provide some type of "memory." Often you find this memory of the action on a list, a tally, or on a record. The worker may think, "Since I have now completed 25 pieces of the job, I will make a note to that effect on this tally." But he also recognizes that 5 parts had to be rejected and he places these in the

reject box. With the boxes and with his tally, the worker is developing a systems memory that reflects the results he is getting.

Observation: This is the end of the first day on this job. There are nine days left before the entire order must be finished. Is the work going according to plan, or isn't it?

6. FEEDBACK FOR CONTROL

The work day is nearly over. The owner-salesman has been out of the shop during the day. He returns and asks the operator, "How did you make out with today's batch?"

Notice that the boss doesn't wait until the end of the 10-day period to see how the job was progressing. He checks it at the end of the first day. If the job is not going right, he still has time to take up some slack and meet the schedule date he promised his customer. The operator gives his boss information that, in a system, is feedback. He says: "Boss, I worked on 30 but I spoiled some of them. I think that the good parts are up to standard."

The owner-salesman, who presumably knows more about machining tech-

niques than the worker, walks over to the work station and looks at the parts in the two boxes. These boxes *represent* the worker's real results from time and materials. The boss looks at the tally, too. The figures on the tally are *symbols* of the work results   of data. He examines the five rejects. Then he gives his attention to the good parts and nods his head. He says: "You're right. The 25 are OK, but the 5 rejects definitely are not. Too many bad ones."

This is the manager's evaluation of the results. He is convinced that the operator's reject total is too high.

Next comes the redirection of action. After discussion with the worker, the boss decides that he knows the solution to the excessive number of rejects. He tells the worker: "Tomorrow, Les, use a slower speed on the first half of the cut."

Here is the control feature of a management system; the boss is now redirecting the action. We have now observed the three basic characteristics of a management system:

1. A call for action to get a specific result
2. Establishing memory reflecting those results
3. Reporting on the results

ACTION—MEMORY—REPORT. A true management system has those three aspects built into it.

8 RE-DIRECTING ACTION

TOMORROW USE A SLOWER SPEED ON THE FIRST HALF OF THE CUT.

At the end of the second work day, the boss can again check the progress of the job. Did the slower cutting speed reduce the percentage of rejections? Was his diagnosis of the trouble correct?

How about productivity? Is the operator turning out enough of the flexible couplings per day to match both the cost and the schedule standard? A systems report answers such questions and enables the supervisors and managers to control the routine actions.

7. FREQUENCY OF FEEDBACK

Reports flow out of the systems channel at frequent intervals, preventing the action from getting too far off the track.

The boss must see that large losses of time and materials do not occur on a total job. In the machine shop example the manager checked the results the operator obtained at the end of the first day—that is, in one-tenth of the total time of 10 days. The boss didn't ask the worker *how* he did the job. He concentrated first on the *results*. And since those results were not right, *then* he checked on *how* the worker had done his work. Now the boss is in a position to "redirect" the man's action.

Here we can see a typical systems control device. First taking the action, then developing a memory, and last providing information on the results to the manager.

8. AN AIRLINE RESERVATION SYSTEM

An airline's income comes from doing its big job—transporting people and things to their destinations. Like any large organization, an airline uses numerous systems to coordinate the work of its many specialized working people—pilots, stewardesses, ground crews, maintenance workers, dispatchers, reservation people, counter personnel, people, baggage handlers, machinists, flight engineers, weather experts. It also deals with hundreds of travel agents.

Systems must reach the outside of the airline organization itself . . . to other, connecting airlines, to air control organizations such as the Federal Aviation Agency . . . to in-flight route controllers, tower controllers, flight inspectors, flight surgeons, ground controllers, and even airport approach controllers.

Looking at another example of a system in action, consider an airline passenger reservation system. The basic objective of this system is to ensure that the passenger has the transportation he needs on a specific day and at a specific time.

Action in the reservation system starts when the passenger knows he must make a trip. He first contacts his travel agent. The passenger's *need* for transportation is the starting force . . . the system's trigger. In many systems some human need starts the action.

At the other end of this cycle, let's consider that the transaction is complete when the passenger has boarded the aircraft and occupied his reserved seat, and the plane is ready to depart.

As we carry the reservation and ticket sale transaction through the systems cycle, we encounter a cast of at least 10 characters. The work of each person must be coordinated with the work actions of others. The transaction begins its systems activity with the passenger.

Mr. Hubbard is a businessman who works in San Francisco. However he makes frequent business trips to Chicago and to New York. A week before he plans a trip, Mr. Hubbard tells his secretary:

Helen, please get me a first-class flight reservation for New York early Monday morning. I'd like to return Wednesday morning as early as I can.

In addition to Mr. Hubbard and his secretary, the following characters will also play a role in this systems transaction:

1. Travel agent
2. Travel office typist
3. Airline reservation clerk
4. Computer center
5. Agent at counter
6. Security guard
7. Agent at gate
8. Stewardess

Now let's follow the action sequence by using the *Playscript * procedure format*.

Actor	Action
Mr. Hubbard	1. When he knows a trip is necessary, asks the secretary to get an airline reservation.
Secretary	2. Phones the request to the travel agent.

* Playscript, a procedure format developed by the author, is now widely used in business and government because it is easy to write and easy to read.

Actor	Action
Travel agent	3. Consults airline guide, selects Atlantic's flight 140 for the out trip and Atlantic's 141 for the return.
	4. Contacts Atlantic's reservation center.
Atlantic's reservation clerk	5. Queries the flight inventory computer for flights 140 and 141 and the days requested, asking, "Is a first-class seat available?"
Computer	6. Checks its inventory memory on flights 140 and 141 on Monday and Wednesday.
	7. Finds seats are available on both flights, so answers "yes."
Reservation clerk	8. Reserves one seat for each flight for Mr. Hubbard.
Computer	9. Reduces seat inventories on both the flights by one first-class seat.
Reservation clerk	10. Advises travel agent that Mr. Hubbard's reservations are confirmed.
Travel agent	11. Directs typist to make up the tickets.
Travel office typist	12. Types up the tickets for both outgoing and return trips.
	13. Mails tickets to Mr. Hubbard's company, along with an invoice.
Secretary	14. Upon receipt of the tickets, gives to Mr. Hubbard.
	15. Marks invoice "Received" and forwards to accounts payable department.

Meanwhile, at the computer reservations center . . .

Actor	Action
Computer	15a. After it decreases by one seat the first-class seat inventories for flights 140 and 141 on the days requested (step 9), the machine stores new balance on a disk memory, preparing for subsequent inquiries for reservations on flights 140 and 141.
	15b. Sets up passenger record on Mr. Hubbard.
	15c. Prepares passenger list (manifest) sets and meal orders and other detailed action notices required to serve the people who will also travel on these flights.

On the day of the trip . . .

Actor	Action
Passenger Hubbard	16. Takes tickets with him to airport.
	17. Lines up before airline's check-in counter.
	18. Presents his tickets, and two pieces of luggage, to counter agent.
Counter agent	19. Checks Mr. Hubbard's name on passenger list.
	20. Takes off the out-trip ticket from Hubbard's book.
	21. Makes up envelope boarding pass, writing in gate number and boarding time, stamps to validate.

Actor	Action
	22. Checks Hubbard's luggage. Staples baggage stubs on boarding pass envelope.
	23. Returns boarding pass and remainder of ticket set, with luggage stubs, to Mr. Hubbard.
Passenger Hubbard	24. Walks to security area to check through.
Security guard	25. Checks Mr. Hubbard and carry-on briefcase.
Passenger Hubbard	26. Walks on to departure gate for check-in.
	27. Lines up at gate counter.
Gate agent	28. When Hubbard presents boarding envelope and trip tickets, checks off Hubbard's name on *his* copy of the passenger manifest.
	29. Offers a seat selection, marking it on the boarding pass.
Passenger Hubbard	30. Sits down to wait in the boarding area.
Gate agent	31. Calls the flight for boarding.
Passenger Hubbard	32. Boards the aircraft.
Stewardess	33. Checks boarding pass envelope, directs Hubbard to his reserved seat.
Passenger Hubbard	34. Takes seat, puts his hat and coat in overhead rack, sits down and buckles seat belt ready for departure.

(End of this systems cycle)

Of course a dozen other systems had to be operating simultaneously, coordinated with this straightforward reservation system, to provide the transportation Mr. Hubbard needs. Some of the related systems include the following:

1. The crew calling and check-in system
2. The mechanical and instrument check system of the aircraft
3. The refueling system
4. The ground handling system
5. The baggage handling system
6. The system for cleaning and resupplying the aircraft
7. Flight route planning
8. Food provisioning if meals are to be served
9. The aircraft airworthiness inspection system
10. The auxiliary power and air conditioning system to be used while the aircraft is parked at the departure gate

If action in one of these related systems fails, then where are you? For example, one support system we may not have accounted for is the airplane cleaning and resupply activity. What will Mr. Hubbard think if he comes into the aircraft and finds spilled food on the seat, or the pocket attached to the back of the seat in front of him is crammed with used drinking cups?

We may take all these services for granted but they don't just happen. People and their systems make them happen . . . by playing their specific work roles in their particular systems. Each of these systems must be neatly and carefully coordinated, one with the other. When the aircraft is ready for departure (it is nosed in at the gate, since a caterpillar ramp is in use), the mechanical "mule" is needed to push the aircraft out in the clear where it can maneuver on its own. If the mule operator fails to show up for work, what happens?

The degree of delicate timing and coordination between all these systems is such that the operating people alone could never devise them . . . and get them coordinated. You get "fine-tuned" systems when you have the guidance of a skilled analyst . . . or a whole crew of them.

We have been considering only one system, one that an airline organization couldn't do business without under today's heavy departure and arrival schedules across the nation and around the world.

Observe that while the system makes use of one of the advanced technical tools available to any system—a large-capacity computer—it is still the people in the systems drama who get the action. They use the computer as a memory tool . . . and as a control tool.

Could such a system operate on a manual basis? On today's transaction quantity scale, it simply is not conceivable.

The action we just described went along rather smoothly. The plane departed on time and each of the subcycle systems, support systems, and parallel systems functioned properly.

But the reservation and boarding passenger phase of the systems cycle does not always go smoothly. We could encounter variations and exceptions. When you do a large amount of business, some deviation, some exceptions are inevitable . . . and you've got to be ready for them. How would you handle the following situations:

1. Passenger requires a stopover at an intermediate point.
2. Passenger must use three different airlines to get to his ultimate destination.
3. Passenger doesn't show up.

4. Departure gate must be changed.
5. Passenger wants to take a later or an earlier flight.
6. Mechanical problems delay the aircraft's departure.
7 Blind passenger arrives with a seeing eye dog.
8. Because plane arrives late at intermediate airport, passenger misses connection.
9. Baggage doesn't arrive.
10. Passenger cancels trip.
11. Standby passenger (no reservation).
12. Wait-listed passenger.
13. Passenger appears drunk.
14. Passenger can't walk.
15. Passenger is very elderly.
16. Passenger is a child.
17. Passenger doesn't speak English.
18. Passenger brings a pet dog without a travel kennel.
19. Passenger requests military, clergy, or student fare.
20. Wants family plan fares.
21. Reservations are duplicated.
22. Passenger has reservation but no ticket.
23. Seat assignments duplicated.
24. Baggage is overweight or oversize.
25. Flight is full and oversold. Four passengers with reservations are left at gate.
26. Passenger leaves personal belongings on aircraft.
27. Travel ticket is lost.

Each variation requires some type of systematic action. You can't leave it to an employee's discretion. The airline employee who has to handle the problem needs an approved path to follow. This may be a subsystem or perhaps a policy guide. He may have to take up a question with his boss, the nearby supervisor.

Consider just one of those subsystems, that of handling personal items that passengers leave on the plane, such as coats, cameras, books, hats, jewelry, packages, briefcases, umbrellas, walking sticks, and crutches.

Other items found when passengers leave include wigs, broaches, raincoats, tennis rackets, golf clubs . . . even eyeglasses, dark glasses, and false teeth. Sometimes women, who take their shoes off for comfort, forget to put them on when they leave the aircraft, presumably walking out into the terminal in their travel slippers.

The discovery by one of the airline employees of the article the passenger left on the aircraft triggers the subsystem we call "Lost and Found." The objective of this system is, of course, to return the article to its owner. Failing that, there must be another system that provides a way to dispose of the article. It may be titled "Salvage of Unclaimed Articles."

CHAPTER 3

THE CLASSIC ROUTE TO SYSTEMS IMPROVEMENT

1. The tried and proven path to a better system
2. Involve the operating people
3. Studying a natural system
4. How a systems study starts
5. Systems improvement steps

Your first step in developing a new and better system is to know what is happening now—in the present system. Rarely will you be called to develop a system that is not already at work.

Your organization's present functions are ongoing. Your organization is now buying, selling, paying, collecting, reporting, storing, sending, and receiving. And the operating people are now using various systems to carry on that work.

1. THE TRIED AND PROVEN PATH TO A BETTER SYSTEM

How does an analyst create a new system, one that is better than the present one? There *are* different ways. Some analysts take an engineering approach to systems improvement. This is the route followed by industrial engineers as they make improvements in the physical systems of factories.

Other men and women see systems improvement as paperwork analysis: "Design better forms, reduce the quantity of forms and you will have better systems." Yet others tackle the improvement job by means of methods work: "Improve each work station and you will have a better system."

Still another way is to measure work output. How much work are the people doing now? How much work could they do if the work was simplified or the individual jobs enriched by making each person's work more comprehensive?

There is a school of thought that maintains that the best approach is to ignore the present system, mentally create an ideal system, describe it, and then compromise downward from that peak of efficiency to get a system that is workable.

Other ways to better systems include procedures improvement, layout analysis, predetermined time standards, incentive arrangements, cost cutting, and even revising the organization's structure ("Let's try shifting the supervisors around."). Meanwhile the computer enthusiast smiles happily: "Let's improve it by putting it on the computer!"

There are merits in any approach to systems improvement. Any improvement should be better than none. But you can't take all these routes at once. You must make your choice. What route should *you* take to improve a system?

Our advice is to follow our *classic* route. It has always worked for us. It always works for others. Many of the other approaches are too dependent on the unique skills, training, or systems development experience of the analyst. However any intelligent person can succeed if he chooses the classic route and follows it deliberately and carefully. So let's briefly describe the classic route:

The analyst studies the present system, analyzes the facts, redesigns the system, and installs it, replacing the present system.

What are some of the characteristics of a new system developed by following the classical route? The analyst first gains a clear understanding of the present systems. The systems users are always involved. The techniques for developing operating people's *acceptance* play a major role. All data requirements of all people are considered and provision is made for them. The action channel is relatively direct.

The analyst recognizes and provides for the main line of action. Following the classic route, the analyst considers peripheral factors that can adversely affect the system. Such factors as these can clog the systems channel or hamper the main line:

Untrained operating people	Incorrect policies
Weak supervision	Poor physical layout
Managerial ignorance of the technical side of the activity	Wrong working environment
	Lack of equipment
No planning	No knowledge of what pro-
Lack of reasonable discipline	ductivity should be

2. INVOLVE THE OPERATING PEOPLE

Perhaps the most important factor in the classic route's frequent success is the analyst's recognition that systems development is basically a *people art*. The people who run the new system must accept it. If they do not, no matter how well the system is planned, engineered, and designed, it is in trouble, computer or no computer.

During your systems study you will be seeking definitive facts. But you need to be almost equally conscious of attitudes. Certainly the new system must be technically sound. But equally important you must secure the support of the operating people. And by following the classic route you will get the people "coming along" with you.

In later chapters various aspects of the classic route come into focus. That is the purpose of this book: to guide you along the classic route to systems improvement. After you know this route and have experienced success using it, you'll be ready to consider alternate routes, or certain aspects of them. All have merit.

Note: In our discussions we use the terms *study* and *survey* interchangeably.

3. STUDYING A NATURAL SYSTEM

It is likely the system you are going to study is a natural rather than a planned system. What is a natural system?

Reminder: Wherever people are active and working together in an organization, they work out some sort of a system, without the help of an analyst. Through these systems the people get their day-to-day work done—buying, selling, making, growing, sending, shipping, transporting, paying money, collecting money, and so on.

If the system behind each of those activities has never been studied or redesigned, the system itself is a natural or home-grown system. Or it could be that the system was designed years ago and is so changed from "patching" that even the original designer wouldn't recognize it. Here's how a natural system develops: the working people, after bumping against each other, finally settle down into workable routines. They say, "You do this," . . . "I will do that," . . . "No, Joe will do that."

Such natural systems do work, but they are wasteful. They use excessive time and materials, use people skills wastefully, cost too much money, and

Intelligent employees, knowing that their respective jobs are interrelated, rig up a "natural system."

soak up supervisory attention because of constant breakdowns. One crisis arises after another. Expediting is common.

In the natural system mistakes are made frequently. People cover them up, though, and higher management does not know how many mistakes are being made.

In a natural system some people routinely redo incomplete or shoddy work done by others. Natural systems are heavy with paper shuffling. Anybody can add a form or a record. Bootleg or "thoughtless" forms often outnumber the official numbered forms. And although people may groan about their paper-work loads, they do not know what to do about it.

So if only natural systems are in use there is a serious weakening of management's power to get results. Productivity (the man-hours consumed in relationship to the value of the output) is low. Thus the entire organization is weakened, threatening the interests of investors, creditors, customers, owners, managers, supervisors, and the operating employees themselves.

Here's an assumption that isn't always accurate: When you put a system on a computer, it is always a planned, not a natural system.

Not necessarily, even though data processing people do some cleanup before they put a natural system on the computer. The machines cannot handle the messy natural system the way people can. But cleaning up and defining the detailed steps of a system sufficiently to put it on the computer doesn't mean that the system is really well planned. It may grade as a "fair" system but not as a good, an excellent, or a great system. Computer technicians do the cleanup, so then we have merely automated a *natural* system.

When capable analysts do the job, the result is a better system, one that is an *automated* as well as a *planned* system.

The losses from using natural systems can be summed up in one word . . . waste. People can see waste when it involves physical items such as food, soil and water, or trees, lumber, and other materials. They cannot see waste in a system because neither the system nor its waste is visible.

The purpose of a systems study is to make that system visible. Only when you can see the present system clearly can you take a "critical look" and say:

This system gets a specific result. The activity in the systems channel is the means of getting that result. What work do the operating people really have to do? What person should do what part of the work? And at what step in the sequence?

How about tools? Do we need all the files, machines, and supplies? When you can see a system, you can convert it from a wasteful *natural* system to a more efficient *planned* system.

When you convert your major systems, your management power and the power of each operating person and each executive who uses that system to manage work will also increase.

4. HOW A SYSTEMS STUDY STARTS

What makes people start a systems study? In some organizations the study starts because there is a computer around with unused capacity. An executive asks, "What else can we put in it?" What other incidents can start (trigger) a survey? Here are some.

Trigger No. 1   A new government law requires a change in a present system, such as payroll.

Trigger No. 2   A letter of complaint from a key customer reaches a top executive.

Trigger No. 3   A department asks for a big increase in its operating funds.

Trigger No. 4   A management consultant (from outside the organization) recommends an internal survey.

Trigger No. 5   An auditor's report uncovers trouble (or potential trouble) in a specific system.

Trigger No. 6   A report on results reaches an executive. He does not like what he reads.

Trigger No. 7   A bottleneck develops. People are alarmed. They say, "Something must be done."

Trigger No. 8   An executive gets an idea from (a) talking to an executive from another organization, (b) reading an article, or (c) listening to a talk on systems.

Trigger No. 9   The systems staff, working on a planned "constant improvement" program, finds that THIS system is the next one scheduled for study (rare).

There are several dozen incidents that could trigger a study. The foregoing are just a few samples.

Top managers should know that natural systems are wasteful. The solution is to assign analysts to study and improve one system after another. They can select the three or four most important systems to work on first. But to begin, they need someone who knows how to identify a system.

5. SYSTEMS IMPROVEMENT STEPS

The aim of anyone studying a system is to develop a good, planned system and then replace the less efficient system. This should eliminate most of the waste found in the unplanned (natural) system.

People use other words to mean *systems study*. Some terms include *feasibility study, survey, systems analysis, survey and analysis, systems development, and systems design.*

When you or someone else studies a system, make sure the work will lead to a better system. To do so, follow these signposts along the classic route to improvement:

Signpost No. 1	The study *trigger*. Ominous symptoms indicate that something is not right. You're not sure what's wrong. Neither is anyone else.
Signpost No. 2	You *explore* the general area. You struggle to get a clear idea of the problem. You search for some definitive facts. Right here you start to bring the operating people into the act . . . going along with you. Ask questions. Explain what you see as the problem. What do they see? At this step you pick up and collect symptoms by the score.
Signpost No. 3	The study *assignment*. After your preliminary investigation, you study the symptoms, sort them, then try to define the problem . . . as you see it *now*.
	You get some idea of the magnitude of the system's activity. This could be the number of transactions per day or per week. Or you may get cost figures. *Two examples:* (1) what does it cost to issue a purchase order and (2) what does it cost to employ a new worker? You may end your study at this point. If the activity is too small, you cannot spend much time to fix it.
Signpost No. 4	*The study of documents:* If you decide to go ahead, you enter the fact-gathering stage. Up to now you have only symptoms (nonfacts) to go on. Before you can analyze the present system, you need factual information about it. You can get information from related documents such as charts, procedures, or computer programs.
Signpost No. 5	*Interviews.* After you squeeze information out of various documents, you arrange the action sequence on a grid (see Chapter 5) chart. With this in hand, you again contact the people in the system. Show them the chart and get their ideas on what should be done. Interview the key people, both operators and supervisors.

Signpost No. 6   *Analysis.* This is the taking-apart step, the sifting and sort-ing of facts. Have the operating people help here. Let them in on the analysis. They'll enjoy it.

Signpost No. 7   *Meditation.* This is the lone-wolf stage. You must do this by yourself. Here you mentally digest the information you have gathered and analyzed. You call on your power-ful subconscious mind to help you see (1) what the sys-tem *is* and (2) what it *should* be.

Signpost No. 8   *Synthesis or redesign.* Your ideas and other people's ideas for a better system start to emerge. Together you and the "improvement team" mentally rebuild what you mentally took apart. This is a big job that involves plans, over-views, and many details.

Signpost No. 9   *The pin pricks (testing).* Let people who understand or run the present system shoot at the new ideas. Will these ideas work? Listen. Be grateful if these people save you from blunders. These criticisms are the healthy "pin pricks" that help ensure that the new plan is sound in most details. No thin skins wanted here.

Signpost No. 10   *Presentation.* Your objective at this stage is to get man-agement approval of your plan for the new system. If you are a member of management, coordinate the new plan with your peers or with the people running the present system.

Signpost No. 11   *Installing the new system.* What must be done? Retain operating people? Rewrite procedures and computer pro-grams? Design and order forms? Order machines, equip-ment, or supplies? Now you plan. Buy new software. You schedule all details. Who will do which job? By when? Through all this planning keep in touch with your project team members. You must serve as a skilled proj-ect manager at this stage. (Many systems projects have gone up on the rocks at this point because of lack of proj-ect management skills.) A big word for this stage is "im-plementation."

Signpost No. 12   *Report on actual results.* After the new system has been operating for four or five months, ask, "How many bene-fits does the new planned system provide that the older system failed to provide?" Were the specific benefits you expected actually achieved? Usually a new system has to run for a time, often as long as six months, before it yields the full benefits.

These steps make up the "classic path" to systems improvement. This path is the one we recommend. It works well for any type of system, in any type of organization, for systems on or off the computer, on large or small systems.

CHAPTER 4

PLANNING THE SURVEY

Since a systems survey is classed as *project* work, not as *routine* work, planning is essential to your success. To plan you need some facts. These facts and the plan itself will change as you go along.

1. YOUR FIRST LOOK

Before you start your full-scale study, take a quick, preliminary look at the situation. Is the request for survey valid as it originally came to you? Or is it merely an indication of trouble quite different from that first report? It may not be systems trouble at all. Often the executive who requested the study is not sure what is wrong. But he is certain that he wants something done about it. So first do a little work to discover the real "it."

You can find out more about the problem by a bit of reconnaisance. Go out into the working area that is affected. Contact the supervisor there and a few of the well-informed operating people. Ask a few questions. If several operations are involved, you could spend from 10 to 15 minutes talking to a number of people. You will find most of them are quite ready to tell you about their troubles.

If the system pivots around a computer, by all means contact the data processing people. Talk to the director, the analyst, the programmer, and the operator. What do they see as the problem?

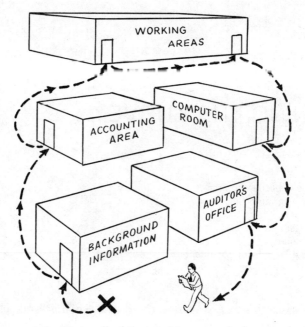

Explore around the "edges" of the problem area before beginning your actual study.

2. SYMPTOMS WILL BUBBLE UP FIRST

When the people you have questioned talk about the problem, most of what you'll uncover will be symptoms. Accept this information as symptoms, not necessarily as facts. Do not judge accuracy at this stage. Here are some things you may hear people say:

If we could only get more help, we could . . .
He didn't know that . . .
The workload is simply too heavy . . .
Paperwork is getting us down . . .
The trouble is over there in the claims department . . .
Costs are out of sight . . .
We told them but they won't listen . . .
The new gals in the department make most of the errors . . .
Nobody knows what caused this . . .
We think the errors occur because . . .

As you first talk to people you'll probably gather symptoms. Accept them. Write them down.

Don't brush symptoms aside. Accept them. Accept them all. They are not necessarily causes, but they could be indicators that will help you find the underlying cause of the trouble.

Some of the symptoms may also be actual causes. Usually they are surface manifestations of a deeper cause. So do listen to people who offer symptoms. Write them down. Encourage the operating people to spill their troubles.

As you talk to people, ask yourself: "How big is this problem? If I go on, could I be spending more (in time) than any correction of the problem could be worth to my organization?"

It is easy to get sucked into an activity that someone thinks you should study. As soon as you know the real problem, ask yourself:

How much study effort is this problem worth?

You cannot afford $100 worth of time to solve a $50 problem. Actually you cannot afford to spend $100 in solving a $500 problem. Unless other factors govern the importance of the study, plain old dollar economics must govern.

The hours that you plan to expend on a survey and on the redesign of the system should promise to pay substantial dividends.

The study of a system can take a couple of hours. It can take a couple of days. Or several years.

3. AIM AT THE ASSIGNMENT

As you gather numerous symptoms and as you think about the size of the problem, aim at the survey assignment. The assignment is one of the identifi able signposts along the classic route to systems improvement. You would think that the systems manager, or the executive who requested the systems study, would give you (the analyst) a specific assignment. They rarely do.

What an analyst gets at first is a vague, unclear problem. It is his job to explore the situation sufficiently to identify the problem (usually) and the systems cycle where the problem lies.

The preliminary look could take a few hours, or even a day or two. It is possible that the real problem will not be uncovered in this preliminary exploration stage. Because of this possibility, the analyst always speaks of the "apparent problem."

By the time the analyst has gathered several dozen symptoms, he will have a pretty good idea of what the problem is.

The problem may not be a systems one at all. It could be one of *poor policy . . . inadequate planning . . . untrained employees . . . incorrect organization structure . . . poor layout . . . poor morale . . . the impact of competition . . . bad pricing . . .* or *weak supervision.*

There *may* be nothing wrong with the present system. Perhaps for some reason people are not using the present system.

The problem may be a nonsystems bottleneck, high costs, a drop in quality, a loss of managerial control, excessive overtime, poor customer service, a new legal requirement, a breakdown of discipline, damaging deviations from policy, dilapidated error controls, obsolete equipment, or conflicting financial reports. . . .

> The problem that is well-stated is half-solved.
> —*John Dewey*

4. THE ASSIGNMENT

On a one-page document, write out all you know about the present problem, covering the following areas:

☐   1. The apparent problem.
☐   2. The systems cycle * within which it lies.

* A logical "package" of one segment of systematic activity, such as the payroll systems cycle.

☐ 3. A few figures on the "order of magnitude":
>   *a.* How many transactions?
>   *b.* How much money?
>   *c.* How many people?
>   *d.* How many computer programs?
>   *e.* How much time?

☐ 4. How much time do you propose to spend on the study?

☐ 5. If you redesign the system, what are the probable benefits? Include both the tangible and intangible gains.

☐ 6. How much total time (all man-hours) do you estimate the study and analysis phase will take?

☐ 7. What is the SPAN of time for completing the study, redesigning, and making a proposal? Ninety days? Six months? A year?

☐ 8. Is the study to be on a team basis? Should someone else be on the team, full time?

☐ 9. A tentative schedule for the completion of the work by phases such as (1) fact gathering . . . (2) analysis . . . (3) redesign . . . (4) proposal . . . (5) scheduling . . . (6) retraining . . . (7) installation . . . (8) testing.

☐ 10. What financial resources (budget) will you need, other than time? Travel? Consultant's fees? Temporary extra help?

☐ 11. What are some of the major symptoms you've picked up so far?

The assignment is a document the analyst uses to coordinate the plan for his work on the system.

When you've organized and written down the most significant facts, you are ready to recheck with the executives who are concerned. Take the assignment to these people and go over it briefly. Each man should get a copy of the assignment. But do not *send* it to him, take it personally. The assignment is not intended to stand alone. It is a tool you use to get agreement on the project you're ready to plunge into . . . the study and improvement of the system. You assignment is a coordination document:

> If all agree, you're ready to go ahead with the study. If some do not agree, find it out now.

If your boss says, "That's about it, go right ahead," then you're on your way. You have an understanding of what you're going to tackle . . . and misunderstandings should be at a minimum.

5. TOUCHING BASE

Your job of improving a system is usually triggered by a problem that certain executives want solved. In the process of solving that problem, you'll encounter other weaknesses in the system. And you'll try to eliminate these as well as to remove the original problem. As the work moves along you'll touch base with these executives at least four times:

1. When the executives ask you to LOOK INTO an unsatisfactory situation.
2. When you recheck with them by giving them a written study ASSIGNMENT.
3. When you PROPOSE to install the newly designed system.
4. After the new system has settled down, when you tell them what the actual results were.

If the job is likely to be a long one, you should give your key executives a progress report at least once a month. Remember:

☞   A systems analyst works *for* management people to improve the systems aspect of the management process.

6. STARTING THE STUDY

What is the next signpost? The inexperienced analyst often says to himself: "Well, now I'll go out there and talk to the people who work in and who know about the current system."

Wrong. That is characteristic of an untrained (amateur) analyst. Before you start interviewing, learn all about that system *other than* by asking people! Your sources of facts about the present system are:

1. Information now on paper.
2. Information in the heads of people.

Your approaches to these two fact-gathering areas must be different. The systems professional considers the two sources something like this:

1. THE SAFE AREA. This is the impersonal and nondelicate process of digging information out of pertinent documents.

DOCUMENT PROBING IS SAFE

To get information about the system, start with documents, not people.

2. THE UNSAFE AREA. This is the highly personal and delicate process of getting information from the people currently working within the system.

In your eagerness to get the study going, you might ride roughshod over people. You can get into trouble by not recognizing the emotional phenomena that we call human feelings.

Most of us are rather clumsy when it comes to face-to-face contacts with people in the system. But if we recognize our weakness in this aspect of our work, we're less likely to get into trouble.

If you recognize that each interview can be explosive, you are more likely to exercise greater care.

PROBING BY INTERVIEWING
CAN BE DANGEROUS. TAKE CARE.

Tread lightly when you set out to interview people.

7.   GET YOUR FIRST FACTS FROM DOCUMENTS

What kind of documents will help you to "see" the present system? Consider
the following:

☐   1. *Auditors'* reports on the original problem.
☐   2. Related operational *reports*.
☐   3. *Accounting* reports.
☐   4. Previous *special studies* on the problem or on the area of activity.
☐   5. Minutes of *staff meetings* where the problem has been discussed.
☐   6. *Organization charts* of the departments involved in the system.
☐   7. Stationery stockroom records on *quantity* of withdrawals of related
       forms used in the system.
☐   8. If you have a reports control program, look at the *reports control*
       records.
☐   9. Work *measurement* records.
☐ 10. *Quality* records maintained by the department. How many errors in a
       period? What type of errors?
☐ 11. Employee *suggestions* about work improvements in this area.
☐ 12. Customer *complaints*, if any.
☐ 13. *Performance standards* in the area.
☐ 14. *Industrial engineering reports* on the activity.
☐ 15. *Written procedures, job outlines,* or *work instructions* currently in use.

☐ 16. Sample *filled-in forms*.
☐ 17. *Memos* or *letters* written about the problem.
☐ 18. *Documents* from the computer area.

Read through these papers quickly. Make notes as you go. Number each note. Then mark up your copies of the source papers with the related numbers. If you're reading the auditor's report first, make that document no. 1. Make notes on a separate sheet of paper, numbering these notes no. 1. When you wind up with 50 or 100 individual notes, you can easily find the source document.

Is there a written procedure that reflects the present system? If so, it is important to your understanding of the system. This is true even if the procedure isn't up to date. So get a copy of it. (There may be several related procedures.) The document may not be called a procedure. It may be a "standard operating instruction," a "methods bulletin," or something similar. Read it. These are the first two questions to ask:

1. What starts the activity? A sale? A request? A claim? (You're looking for the *trigger*.)
2. What is the result of this systems activity?

When you have identified those two points, you have "bracketed" the cycle of the system you are studying.

The procedure can yield much information about the present system. Who does what specific work? At what work station? In what department? In what sequence?

What action forms (orders, etc.) does the procedure mention? Does it refer to any records or reports? Any computer programs? Does it mention any individual instructions such as those people use to train an employee to use a data terminal?

How accurate is that procedure? Does it reflect what is happening in that system today? You don't know. You will not know until you have completed your study.

This much you do know about the procedure: In the past, someone wrote it and meant it to reflect the system. Much thought went into it. This is true whether the procedure is well or badly written.

After you have charted the procedure's action as best you can, gaps and omissions will become apparent. How did the action move from process step 11 (in the scheduling office) to process step 12 (in the parts stockroom)? Make a note of such a gap. You can fill in those omissions later when you talk to the people.

With the procedure and its graphic reflection on a grid chart (see Chapter 5), you can now relate the other information to the systems channel. The procedure can be compared to the keel of a vessel. Once you have it laid out, you can add the other members such as the ribs.

Auditor's reports, committee minutes, policies, reports, complaints, memos, measurements . . . these yield information that begins now to fit in . . . to fill out the puzzle. The murky haze you first saw around the problem begins to clear a little.

CHAPTER 5

FINDING THE SHAPE
OF THE SYSTEM

A management system is not visible. Most of its elements are also intangible. That makes it hard to describe. To many people in the organization the system is either a computer, a manual, or something incomprehensible . . . maybe it's another name for accounting.

1. "TAKE A PICTURE": USE A CHART

We use many types of charts in communicating information. Most charts cannot picture an entire system: only a flow chart can accomplish this. We have numerous types of flow charts, including process charts, block sequence charts, computer logic charts, paperwork flow charts, and physical (layout) flow charts. However, the flow chart that shows the system best is the grid flow chart.

2. ELEMENTS OF THE GRID CHART

The grid chart takes its name from its resemblance to the strips across a football field . . . the gridiron.

With a grid chart you can produce a picture of the system's channel, from its origin (trigger) to its result. The major elements of a grid chart include:

1. The field of action . . . the grid
2. The people involved: the actors who do the work
3. Short descriptions of the work that these people do
4. Flow lines that indicate how the individual jobs are linked together into the team play
5. Bold numbers that show the sequence of the processing steps within the system's channel

Here is an example of a grid chart.

Grid Chart

Name of System: Fulfilling Customer's Orders				Date: 12/20/75	
Broker	Warehouse		Shipping Department	Billing Department	Accounts Receivable
	Warehouseman	Packer			
① Takes order from customer on form 87, ORDER ② Sends order to Warehouse	③ Pulls Materials ④ Gives to packer with Order	⑤ Prepares materials for shipment ⑥ Stencils address on boxes ⑦ Sends to Shipping	⑧ Loads on truck ⑨ Notifies Billing by sending "filled" order.	⑩ Prepares form 42 INVOICE, from form 87 ORDER ⑪ Mails original & duplicate to customer ⑫ Sends parts 3 & 4 to Accounts Receivable	⑬ Sends Commission copy to Broker ⑭ Upon Receipt of invoice sets up aging file
⑬A Receives commission copy of invoice					

3. IDENTIFY THE BRACKETS OF THE SYSTEM

You have selected a system for attention. Now determine the exact extent of that system, as well as the activities that take place within the system's channel.

Before you consider all the work that is done within the channel, bracket that system by finding two key points:

1. The transactional trigger
2. The result of the activity

These two points are the enclosures of your system. It is true that in every organization there are networks of systems having dozens of channels or cycles. Many of these are connected to other systems. To improve a system, you must chop off these connections at some point. Otherwise you could go on

Bracket the channel of the system you're studying. Pin down the trigger (start) and the result (end).

studying indefinitely and never improve a single system. Here are some typical systems brackets:

Transactional Triggers	*Results from Systems Action*
1. Purchase order mailed to vendor	1. Goods delivered
2. Goods received	2. Stock replaced
3. Invoice received	3. Check sent
4. Employment application	4. Employee hired
5. Request to hire	5. Employee starts to work
6. Goods shipped	6. Customer invoiced
7. Billing	7. Money collected
8. Claim received	8. Claim settled

What major types of work does your organization do? Sell? Insure? Serve? Manufacture? Store? Ship? Transport? Educate? Control or regulate? Handle claims? Each type has at least one system that people use to get work done. In manufacturing there are dozens of systems.

Many of the systems that you will study and improve are related to other systems. *Examples:* An inventory system will relate to a procurement system, which relates to receiving systems, which relates to an accounts payable system.

In a large organization each activity is always a separate system. The respective triggers would be low stock, a request, a receipt of goods, and an invoice. But in the small organization (10 to 100 employees), the analyst may decide to treat all three as one cycle. Then the trigger would be low stock and the result would be stock replacement, treating payment as a subsystem.

4. ISOLATE AND IDENTIFY YOUR SYSTEM

Your objective is to get a view of the system that contains the problem you're going to solve. Naturally you'll also realize that there are connecting systems. OK. Make a note of these connections; otherwise ignore them . . . for now. If you try to study the entire network of systems in the organization, your study effort could run for years.

A system is a working arrangement. A number of people (at least two) get work done on a coordinated or teamwork basis. You are now asking "What is the logical package of such work in *this* system?"

The system is invisible until you study it and give it tangible form.

Observation: The selection of a logical systems cycle (with its channel) is an art, not a technique or a science. You have to decide. Even the number of identifiable work steps required to carry out the transaction and get the result are not always a measure of the extent of the cycle. It may help if you consider my experience. I have found that the many logical cycles I have selected and have worked on have run from about 10 identifiable steps to as high as 50. That doesn't mean that there couldn't be a logical systems cycle of 4 or 5 steps . . . or an equally logical one of 60 or 80 steps.

The majority of systems that include more than 50 identifiable work stations * rate another look. Would it be better if you broke such a system into two cycles, which will remain connected? If the problem lies within the first 25 steps, not in the last 25, perhaps you should break the system apart (mentally, of course) at step 25.

5. FIRST FIND THE TRIGGER

To see your system's shape, first ask, "What triggers the action in this system?" That is the start of the cycle . . . the trigger. If you have ever worked

* This does not apply to the tiny work steps contained in a computer program, which can include hundreds or even thousands of work statements.

HOW DO YOU GET THE INFORMATION?

TRANSACTIONS ORIGINATE HERE

BY PHONE. THEN I FILL OUT FORM 638 AND CHECK AGAINST THIS PRINTOUT.

Start your study at the logical beginning of the system—at the work station where the transactions originate.

around a storeroom or warehouse, you know that there is a withdrawal system. Each time someone walks off with one type of stock, a stock clerk (or a computer) deducts the quantity withdrawn from the balance on hand, shows a new balance, and asks:

Is the balance now down to the reorder point (down to the reserve supply)?

Example: If the balance before that last withdrawal was 500 and the quantity withdrawn is 110, the new balance is 390. Then the clerk (or the computer) looks at the reorder point quantity. If it is 400, the person (or the machine) writes or prints out a "requisition on Purchasing." This is an action form. It represents a replacement transaction. The clerk puts the form into the systems channel, and it flows through to the buying department. Thus the replacement *transaction* is on its way.

Think of each system as providing a channel (cycle). The various transactions (in this example, represented by a purchasing requisition) flow through this channel, one after the other, day after day, like a series of barges going down a river.

6. WHAT IS THE SYSTEM'S OBJECTIVE OR RESULT?

At the far end of the system's channel is a *result*. What is it? Write it down. If you can't write it, it isn't clear to you. (The "objective" of a system is the same thing as a result.)

As you study the present system you will find that people are carrying on a great deal of activity. Most of the people doing work know what their jobs are and what their duties are. They don't always see the objective (the systems result) of the sum total of their work. *You* must see it. When you have an absolutely clear vision of the transactional trigger and of the work objective (result) of the system, you have done much to make that system clear.

Don't neglect those two factors, trigger and result.

Both the trigger and the result or work objective must be absolutely clear to you. To be certain that they are clear, write them down and let people look at them. Do the others agree with you? Is the point you have selected truly the trigger, or can the action start in other ways? Is your second point truly the work objective? Are the results you have identified really those that are obtained from the work? People may give you information that is really the naming of *sub*objectives.

For example, the real objective of a payroll system is simply to pay the employee. But people often get locked in on all the subobjectives of a payroll system such as keeping records on employee's earnings, paying taxes collected through the payroll system, and labor and cost analysis. Those are subobjectives, not the basic systems objective.

To tell the difference, ask: "If this objective were eliminated, would the others still be there?" If you didn't pay an employee, all the subobjectives would be gone too, wouldn't they?

When you move into the design phase of the system (actually the redesign phase), the thinking you have done about the work objective will loom large in your consideration. Knowing the objective will help steer your planning toward the "right answer" for the new system.

Don't be surprised to find that some expensive activity has no clear-cut objective. It is the way that "it" has always been done, and nobody has ever asked why. This is particularly true of natural systems, those that have never really been planned.

Don't think that the system's objective is anything complex. You can spot it and spell it out. It will be something simple like shipping, paying, making, selling, serving, controlling, or filing.

7. THE TRANSACTION: VEHICLE
OF THE SYSTEM

When two men meet and one buys a horse from the other, a transaction has taken place. It is a single unit of business. These "units of business" have not changed for a hundred years, even though we are now using sophisticated techniques to reflect the transactions. Data is not the transaction itself. Data symbolically represents the real transaction.

Today we hear much about files, records, fields, bits, bytes, core positions, characters, words, positions, and partitions. These all relate to data, but they are minor factors in the system. The single real vehicle of the system is the transaction. In a computer system, people put heavy emphasis on the file. But the file is dead unless it is continually brought to life by the transaction.

It is the transaction that is identifiable, the indivisible single unit of business that flows through the system's channel. Each transaction is represented by a cluster of data . . . information that describes that specific transaction.

Description of the transaction starts with the title of the action form that will carry the data. If the title of a form is PURCHASE ORDER, you know that you are looking at a cluster of data that pertains to buying. After the title will come the filled-in data, such as the supplier from whom you are buying, what you are buying, and all the other details that go with a buying transaction.

Each day transactions flow through the various systems, sometimes by the hundreds and even by the thousands. They flow through a specific system's channel.

So the transaction, and the cluster of data that represents it, is the system's common unit. It is the "bit of business" that flows through the system's channel. Control the transactions and you control the routine actions that take place in the system.

8. TIME SPAN IN THE CYCLE

How long does it take a transaction to go through the system's channel? That is, to move from the trigger to the result. Does it take a few hours? A few days? Longer than that? This is the time span of the transaction.

You will be looking for what you regard as the "normal" time span for the transactions that take place in your system. Let's say the norm seems to be approximately 5 days. Then you'll ask, "What are the outside and inside limits of the time span? Could one transaction go through in 3 days? Could others actually take 10 days?

If a shortened time span is an advantage, you might plan the new system to achieve this goal. If you're considering customer service, a faster time span is usually an advantage—a benefit to the customer therefore a benefit to your organization.

9. CAN YOU COST A TRANSACTION?

If you decide what you should include in the cost, you can do a costing job on transactions now and on transactions costs after you install the new system. Every requisitioning transaction, every request for check transaction, every order transaction, every claim transaction, or every buying transaction . . . each can be priced out and costed.

Some organizations have a policy of not accepting an order below a $10 total. You can understand this. If it takes the organization $5 to handle a transaction, it must draw the line somewhere, establishing a minimum or floor on orders.

In one study of transaction costing, we used the purchase order. Analysts from different companies met and discussed their buying costs and how they costed each transaction. The analysts agreed on the factors that would be included in the cost. The lowest figure per purchase order issued was $4.75 each. The highest was $78.07 each. The lower priced transactions were rather simple operations, whereas the higher costs were due to complex factors such as requiring bids and quotations.

CHAPTER 6

BRING PEOPLE ALONG WITH YOU

Want to enjoy the benefits of a really good new system? To do so you need the acceptance of the system by the people who will run it.

Business and governments are today loaded with cold fish systems that turn most people off. Why? Because the designer's thinking has been primarily *technical:* "How can I make this work on the computer?"

1. PEOPLE ARE ESSENTIAL

The few great systems that are running in some organizations are people-oriented systems, not computer-oriented systems. The computer is a great tool, but it is not the most vital element in a system.

 The people who work within the system, who run it day by day, are the SINGLE VITAL ELEMENT

You can have a good system without a machine, but you cannot possibly have a good one without well-informed people to run it.

We stress the people aspect because so many analysts, working to improve a system, have not given much attention to the people factor. And invariably the resulting new system is a disappointment. It does not yield the promised benefits.

Please don't misunderstand. I have the greatest respect for the professional men and women who can and do handle the technical aspects of data processing. Without them, the computer and all the peripheral gear would be useless. I've known programmers and analysts who were not just dedicated people, they were near-geniuses in their field. Data processors are people, too. If we want their help in developing the technical aspects of the system, we should respect them. We must have their acceptance as well as the acceptance of the systems users.

2. TWO REQUIREMENTS FOR SYSTEMS SUCCESS

When you set out to study and then to improve a system, your success will depend on two factors:

1. *Your systems design.* How well did you design the new system to reach its objective? This includes all the technical aspects.
2. *The acceptance of the using people.* People will run the new system. Will they accept it?

Both these aspects must be handled carefully, or your work will end in frustration. An excellent systems design that is unacceptable to the operating people will not achieve all the benefits it could achieve.

Many an analyst has felt that he could solve a problem simply by using the computer. Yes, the computer is an excellent tool . . . probably the greatest machine yet developed by man. Yet it is men and women who get results. They get the work done. They reach the objective. The computer is a helper . . . an aid to the doers, the people. If any machine fails to aid the people in doing their work, then its value is highly questionable.

☞ People are the key to a successful system.

3. PARTICIPATION LEADS
TO ACCEPTANCE

You will have a better new system if the people in the present system *take part in your study*. Let others share the study and design load. At least a part of the responsibility for improving the system should rest on the men and women who use that system.

This does not mean that six or eight people will spend full time on the study. But it does mean you will contact the "work experts" at appropriate points.

The people on the job know there *is* a problem. Talk to one person at a time. What does *he* think is wrong? What does *she* think should be done about it?

Your one-page assignment included something on "participation." How many people will you contact? Who? How? When? Where? What departments are involved?

There are two reasons for working closely with the people who are in the system:

1. You need their knowledge of the work.
2. You need their acceptance.

4. EXTRA DIVIDENDS
FROM PARTICIPATION

The dividends from your careful handling of the participation phases of your study will go beyond this project. The people tend to become "systems minded." They grow to appreciate the reasons for a better system that they helped to achieve. They understand the present system and know what should be changed and why. They become discriminating. They know a good system when they see one.

Each person finds it interesting to see his job as one of a series of essential roles in a specific system. As the picture of the present system emerges, the men and women who run it begin to understand what other members of that same systems team do. They will see how the other work relates to theirs.

Our experience includes systems improvement work both with and without participation. Invariably our best, most enduring systems resulted when we let the real work experts in on the fun.

Even after design and installation, the new system needs to be maintained. Somebody must alter it in minor respects to meet changing requirements. When the people who run the system understand it, changes can be made quickly and easily.

People's understanding of the width and breadth of the system also makes it flexible. Most transactions flow along smoothly. But no system can provide for every exception or every variation. When that inevitable "tough nut" transaction threatens to clog up the action channel, the system's users will know how to handle it.

5. PEOPLE RUN THE SYSTEM

Many managers think that a system is made of data, forms, computers, application programs, terminals, operating systems, memories, access times, logic charts, and detailed charts. If asked, "What is the most important element of the system?" Many people reply, "the computer" or "data."

Not so. Even in countries where the computer is used heavily, probably 90% of the identifiable systems are not even on the computer! It is true that most of the large systems use a computer, but even here the most important element is PEOPLE, not machines.

The most sophisticated computer-using system is dependent on people for its input . . . for using its output . . . for inquiring of its memory.

Example: Airline reservation systems are sophisticated and complex, yet the people and machines react well together. The system, using electronic machines as major tools, is highly responsive to the needs of users . . . airline counter agents, reservation people, travel agents, and passengers.

You are studying a specific system. Your purpose is to eliminate problems that lie within that system's channel. You will redesign the system so that it is smoother, more effective, less wasteful, faster, and cheaper. It can be all those things, yet not be a really good system. Your real aim in redesign are to see that (1) the system's new channel enables transactions to reach the objective (result) directly and swiftly, and (2) the system is *highly responsive* to the people who use it.

6. WHAT ARE PEOPLE LIKE?

Each human being is a living soul, the spiritual and physical work of our Creator. To his fellow humans he is an enigma. Indeed a man does not even understand himself, let alone others.

Since we cannot go deeply into the nature of man or of woman here, our "study" of people must be limited to one objective: to achieve a better system, a system that the people will like to use. Such a system will be responsive to individual's informational needs. With such a limited objective, we have found a few usually workable techniques for handling a job's people aspects. Not always, but usually.

First consider the man *in the present system*. How does he feel about it? He probably has mixed emotions. The system could be better. It could be worse. He has probably learned to live with its weaknesses and its problems. After stewing about the waste or the clumsiness for several years, chances are that he no longer tries to make changes. He probably found that no one really listened. His "flame for improvement" has all but flickered out.

Suddenly there you are. You are studying the present system so that he and you, working together, can redesign it and make it better.

If there are 15 people working in the present system and there will be 15 people in the new system, how will each of them feel about that new system? Will they like it? Tolerate it? Dislike it? Could they want to see it fail?

To make the new system a real winner, what do you need most from these people? How about their *eager acceptance?* Of course. If that's the best, why not get it? Then, even if you have done only a mediocre planning job, their acceptance can ensure a successful new system.

You can (roughly) grade people's attitudes when you put the new system to work.

Attitude No. 1   *Thumbs down*. The new system is a threat to personal status, income, job security, personal importance, prestige. People may work for its failure. (Quiet sabotage.)

Attitude No. 2   *So-so*. They do not think it is any better. Feel some disdain for the new system. Don't really care if it fails or succeeds.

Attitude No. 3   *It's OK*. Acceptance without enthusiasm. Shrugged shoulders. Just another change. Not too bad. Some things are better.

Attitude No. 4   *Enthusiastic acceptance*. When are we going to get it going? Let us get on with it!

Question: How do you avoid people attitude 1? How do you come as close as practical to people attitude 4? How can you stir up *enthusiastic* acceptance?

Answer: Use system-user participation techniques from start to finish!

No matter how well you handle the participation aspects, some people remain unresponsive. Expect it.

Warning: Most good workers cannot wait to see improvements made. But all employees aren't "good workers." You can't get everybody going with you, no matter what you do. Each man and each woman will react differently.

There are always a few people who do not care one way or the other. One of our associate consultants expressed his idea of the unresponsive person this way: "A meatball is a meatball. You will never change him. But there are enough of the salt-of-the-earth type of men and women to give your new system terrific drive if you know how to tap that drive."

So accept the fact that you cannot win over all the people. Do try. And if you do it right, you will get most of the people going with you.

7.   THE MAN IN THE SYSTEM

What does the working man or woman want from the job, consciously or subconsciously? In systems you can deal only with the people's work. You can do little about anyone's frustrated childhood, unhappy love affair, health, family, marital, or financial problems. A greater degree of job happiness is the most that you and the new system can provide. By the manner in which you develop a new system you can:

1. Provide the man on the job with *more enjoyment* from his daily work.
2. Achieve a new system that produces greater results because most of the workers enjoy *using* the new system.

We have been referring to "your" system, and in some places we continue to do so. You are the person with the initiative. You are the spark plug that ignites the systems improvement work. If you or a professional analyst do not push for a better system, the present one will go right on, bumbling along with all its problems and weaknesses. Now, however, the word "our" must be stressed rather than "your." If you succeed in the participation phases of the job, it will be the *users'* system and *your* system, not just yours alone.

This analogy helps clarify the different roles. When an architect designs a house, he does so in close coordination with the homeowner . . . the man who will *live* in that house, who uses its facilities and its features.

In systems improvement work you are the architect. But when you finish your work, the systems owner must *live* in the "systems house" you built together.

8. A MAN'S MOTIVATORS

What motivates a man or a woman to produce results on the job? Pay? Let's examine the question of pay first. If your organization did not pay him, an employee would not come to work. If he considered your pay inadequate, likely he would seek a job elsewhere.

So let us assume that the man's pay, as well as his working conditions, are reasonably satisfactory. What else then does he want from his eight hours of work?

An employee who is motivated does better work and accepts the systems changes that he feels will lead to better teamwork with his fellow workers. From the systems point of view the average employee's five "work motivators" include the following:

1. He is in on what is going on, such as the development of a new system.
2. He enjoys personal identification. He is not just a cog in the wheel.

3. He gets personal satisfaction from doing his work well.
4. When he accomplishes something special, someone he respects expresses the organization's appreciation.
5. As a worker he has the respect of his fellow workers and of his supervisor.

9. IN ON THINGS

The man in the system wants to know what is being planned and how it will affect him. A systems study? He wonders why. A new system? What will it be like?

Do not surprise him with a full-blown plan for a new system. Instead let him in on the fun of creating the new system as early as possible (preferably the first day). Start when you begin your preliminary study of the present system. Respect his working position. Ask him what should be done . . . from his viewpoint.

Let him see your grid chart that "pictures" the present system as you constructed it from documents. Turn it so that he sees it right side up. Point out where his work station column is located on the chart. Ask questions about the work that is stated in his column.

One man who develops new systems always makes 8½ × 11 inch copies of his grid chart. He leaves a copy with every person he talks to. It is likely that in all the years an employee has been on the job, he has never seen a "picture" of the system in which he works.

Some people may seem cold at first. If a worker is slow to come around, recognize what he may have experienced in the past: ideas rebuffed, squelches, defeats, changes that were not improvements . . . even inept leadership.

10. PERSONAL IDENTIFICATION

No self-respecting person wants to be regarded as just another worker. Consider how a successful salesman works with people. He does not lump his prospects as "a hundred or so prospects." He identifies and gets to know *each one*.

Realizing the value of a simple memory device, the salesman puts down a few facts about the prospect (or customer) on a "prospect card." One salesman may call on 100 or more people, but just before a call, he recharges his memory, gleaning the facts about that particular customer from the card.

You can use a similar technique. Use a memory aid such as a detailed card with notes on each key person . . . worker, supervisor, or manager. Ask his supervisor to tell you about him. Then review those notes before you contact the man or the woman.

11. APPRECIATION FOR A JOB WELL DONE

Some people contemptuously brush aside those who do certain forms of work, saying, "Well, he just sweeps the floor . . . he is only a porter."

If you have such an attitude and it comes through to the worker, what happens? In the case of the janitor, your office floor is likely to get a poor job of sweeping. (Would you like to work in an office where the floors are not well swept?) The man who does that work needs appreciation for his accomplishments, just as much as the star salesman.

If the job is sweeping the floor, how much floor footage should a man sweep in an hour? If his supervisor has set up a reasonable standard, and the man reaches or exceeds that standard, does anyone appreciate his accomplishment? If you know of above-average performance, comment on it to the worker.

Show appreciation for people's efforts to do a good job.

12.   RESPECT HIS KNOWLEDGE

If an employee will be affected by a change in the system, use a little time to consult him. A five or ten minute interview may do it. Ask for his views on the effect of any proposed change on HIS part of the work. This shows that you have respect for his work, for his knowledge, and for him as a member of the systems operating team.

Make it clear that you reserve the right to make the final decision, even if it is contrary to his advice. His idea will be one of a number of suggestions that you will consider. And do consider it. If you cannot use it, tell him so and tell him why. A phone call is enough.

If he knows that you have really considered his ideas, the "respect motivator" is at work in him.

Sometimes we think of authority as residing only in supervisors and managers. But workers, too, have authority . . . the authority of the work expert. Do you think a wise manager is going to tell a qualified electrician how to wire a house? Or tell an experienced truck driver how to handle his rig? Or a top secretary how to make operational decisions? He will not, if he really is a manager.

13.   WORK SATISFACTION

Many jobs seem to be dull or uninteresting. If you know how a specific job fits into the systems "drama," do not take it for granted that the person on that job also knows how the job fits. Often he doesn't know.

Interest the employee. Point out how his work contributes to the system's objective. Show how it fits in with other operations. The aim? To increase the man's work SATISFACTION. You can stimulate a new interest in that same job by awakening his interest in the whole plan for systems action.

If you feel that his job is too restrictive now, too specialized, you are in a position to suggest "job enlargement." Propose this to his *supervisor,* not to him.

14.   WHAT PEOPLE LIKE AND DON'T LIKE

Because we who do systems improvement work are people, we have a hard time figuring out the best way to handle other people. No matter how hard we

The man who uses the system, the worker, has certain psychological needs. The system can help to satisfy them.

try, we will be relatively inept at the human relations aspects of the system. But let's resolve to do the best we can. About the most we can hope for is to make ourselves a little *less* inept than we are naturally.

Let's consider some of the things that people like and some of the things they don't like. Of course, there can be exceptions . . . but we have numerous indications that most people like or dislike the following.

He Likes	He Dislikes
☐ 1. To feel needed	☐ 1. Strangers
☐ 2. Recognition	☐ 2. Being ignored
☐ 3. Security	☐ 3. Threats
☐ 4. Togetherness	☐ 4. Criticism.
☐ 5. A chance to talk	☐ 5. Isolation
☐ 6. Having a choice	☐ 6. Soft soap talk
☐ 7. Being in the know	☐ 7. Loss of status

Sometimes, if we try, it is possible to distill 20 years of work experience into a few words, as the following three statements indicate.

1. If you design a good system but the people who operate it do not accept it, that system *will fail*.

2. If you design a fair system and the operating people do accept it, it *will work*.
3. If you design a good system and the operating people accept it, you'll have a system that *will really spin*.

INTERVIEWING PEOPLE

You won't be able to get all the information about the present system from documents. Much of the needed information isn't written. It is in the minds of the people now working within the present system.

To extract that information, you talk to people. You interview them.

1. DOCUMENTS ARE A LIMITED SOURCE

Certainly the documents were helpful . . . the policies and procedures, job outlines, minutes, programs, charts. But they can tell you only from 40% to 50% of what you need to know about the present system.

First discover the system's route from documents. Use interviews to put factual flesh on the bones.

However, after you have exhausted the information that you can comb from related documents, you have a fairly accurate picture of the system. You see the extent of the channel. You know the sequence of the work operations that take place along that channel. You have the two systems cycle brackets in view: you have identified (1) the transactional *trigger,* and you know (2) the *result* of the activity.

From the documents you developed a grid chart showing the sequence in which the system's actors perform their individual work actions. It provides a "picture" of the present system.

Did you notice that the documents did not tell you the entire systems story? There were holes . . . some gaps . . . a lack of connections. So you have a number of unanswered questions. One vital question is this: Is the actual practice at some variance from what the documents indicate?

2. THE CAST OF CHARACTERS

As you start to extract information from people about the present system, recognize that you will be dealing with four different categories of people:

1. The operator, the employee who does the work
2. His or her supervisor
3. The recorders, the clerks who record what other people are doing
4. Staff advisors and helpers

Although in a given department you will not interview everyone who is involved in the system, you will interview a sampling of them . . . certain key people. Start with the worker's supervisor. He is responsible for the work getting done. He can give you quite a bit of information. He may even know intimately the details of the system. Just as often as he does not know the details, but he has an accurate view of the system as it affects his section or his department.

Usually you will have to see one of the key workers to get down to cases on the way the work is now carried on.

You also want to know what is being recorded. What are the clerks and secretaries doing? They may have some impact on the system. Often a supervisor has an assistant, a staff worker, who has done some work on elements of the system. If such a staff person exists, you should talk to him.

3. PURPOSE OF TALKING TO PEOPLE

Interviewing is the next signpost or way station on your classic road to system improvement.

Besides talking to the people who work *in* the system, you will talk to others who are not actually working in the system, such as auditors, accountants, and staff people. Through them you can get background information and clear up some gaps or establish connections. People who do not actually work in the system's channel sometimes can tell you about it.

Interviewing people is a step that provides you with multiple opportunities . . . opportunities that you can seize on to make the new system a superior one.

These opportunities include (1) getting new facts, (2) verifying facts obtained from documents, (3) getting answers to questions that are still open, (4) giving people a chance to get in on the improvement project, (5) bringing new interest to the individual's job, and (6) getting specific ideas on what should be done. Consider these values from interviewing.

1. *Getting new facts.* You will now get information that the documents failed to yield. People in the system *do* know what work is being done. They are the real "work experts." From them you will get both new facts and deeper insights into the problem.
2. *Verifying facts from documents.* Is the information you've gathered so far correct? Obsolete? Half correct and half wrong? Is the current practice the same as the "picture" you obtained? Or does it vary? In what respect?
3. *Getting answers to your "still open" questions.* How does the transaction move from processing point 6 to point 7 in the systems channel? The documents didn't tell. The men and women in the system can help you fill in the holes, make connections, bridge the gaps.
4. *In on things.* Working people want to know what is going on. By discussing the present system with them, you, in effect, invite these people to become members of the systems improvement *team*. This is informal. You invite them just by discussing the present system with them. Tell them what the problem appears to be.
5. *New interest in the job.* You are paying attention to the employee, to his work, and to his job problems. In so doing you help to make his job more enjoyable. By taking part in systems improvement work, the worker can develop a better understanding of the team aspects of the system's channel in which he lives and works.
6. *What should be done?* You are not really ready to decide what should be done. At this time you seek only to *see* the present system. Yet these people *will* give you ideas on what should be done. Even if you do not seek such suggestions at this stage, you will get them. Do not reject them. Accept them. Make a note of them. But do not pass judgment on their worth at this time.

As in any effort, one aim at a time must be paramount. And your aim now, at the interview stage, is to get information about the present system. You are not yet ready to decide what is or is not going to be needed in the new system.

When people offer you such ideas, however, take them. Think of these suggestions as by-products of finding out about the present system. Write the ideas down and date them. Name the suggestor. If you incorporate one of these ideas later (when you redesign the system), credit the man or woman who proposed it. If you do not write down the idea and its author, you are likely to forget. But the person who gave that idea to you *will not* forget. Don't be accused of being a "credit thief."

4. YOUR ROLE

As you contact people, do you make clear exactly what your goal is?

Most people are departmental or "group oriented." They feel an allegiance to their own working group. Often they blame other groups for systems errors or troubles. You, however, are a catalyst . . . the individual who brings various work elements together into a unified plan. But you need partners, people who can contribute ideas and knowledge about the present systems and the present work elements. Your job is to weave together your ideas and the ideas of others.

Hold back on decisions. Don't try to decide what should be done. Not yet. The people themselves tend to do this. And when they do, if the ideas sound reasonable, you should accept them.

Let's use an analogy. The people may be spinners of the yarn (details), but you are the weaver of cloth (the whole).

Before you talk to anybody, get an appointment. Phone or send a short memo. Never interview an operating person without getting the supervisor's approval.

Are you clear on the role that you are to play in this systems improvement study? Do you see the role that the person you will be talking to will be playing? Each is different. You are the "ball carrier." The person in the system is an idea contributor. The initiative comes from you. The men and women who work in the system will react to your initiative.

Think again about the architect-homeowner relationship. The architect can design the house. He can take care of the technical details such as calculating structural strengths and specifying materials. But the homeowner tells how he wants the rooms arranged: where the bedrooms are to be, the dining area, the baths, and so on. He knows what functions (work) will be carried on.

Thus systems improvement work is a joint effort. One person carries the systems improvement "ball" (you). Other people make contributions of various types both to the study and, later, to the redesign of the system.

Note: The people who work in the system can't change it. You can. So you become *their* instrument for making a desirable change.

Your attitude toward workers is most important. A positive attitude starts when you show respect for the work that each individual is doing. And your real attitude will "bubble up" despite any words you use. The more you know about the job and the individual you are going to interview, the more you can develop this attitude of respect. Your attitude must be one of genuine interest.

Certainly you will see things that are "bad" or "wrong." That's why you are working on the system. But don't dwell on these. Avoid all criticism.

Can these people trust you? Will you level with them? Will you be open and honest with them? When they are convinced that you are not working for your own self-interest but for the good of the organization, they will be inclined to trust you. Be extremely careful that you don't shake this trust in any way.

In summary, to prepare yourself for interview:

1. Respect the worker and what he does.
2. Understand your role (initiative).
3. Understand the (contributing) role of the worker.
4. Be honest with the worker. Never play games with him.

5. HOW MUCH SHOULD YOU TALK?

Since you don't know anything except what you've pulled out of documents, talk as little as possible. Make no comments; just ask questions. Explaining something you found in a document is about as far as any of your statements should go.

Questions to the person you are talking to will fall into the two parts, what and why.

Reminder: You are after the facts, but remember too you are after acceptance. Acceptance! ACCEPTANCE!! A C C E P T A N C E ! ! !

The average employee doesn't get much chance to have his say about what is being done. Often this applies to a supervisor whose manager doesn't listen to him. If you can establish his confidence in you as an impartial, helpful, friendly individual, both people (supervisor and worker) are likely to express themselves quite thoroughly.

Some people are so repressed that as you talk to them they boil over and tell you all about the situation as they see it. Others are cautious and quiet. Some are downright fearful.

Don't criticize the present system. You might be talking to the man who put it in.

If you encounter a person who appears to be fearful or apprehensive, tell him why you want the information.

Tread carefully when people tell you about some "sad" situation that you immediately see is wrong. You'll be tempted to make a suggestion then and there. Resist that temptation.

At this stage of the work you must carefully observe the following requirements:

1. Do not criticize anything or anybody.
2. Do not suggest making changes: Just find out what is happening now: Do not give advice or orders.

6.   LISTEN . . . LISTEN CAREFULLY

Speaking is the first half of communication. Listening is the second half. The only way you can extract the wealth of knowhow that resides in the people in the present system is by listening . . . by getting them to talk. On your first contact, therefore, your talking should be 90% questions, and even those should be less than 30% of the total that is being said. Let the systems users do 70 to 80% of the talking.

The people you are talking to now are rich in work experience and knowledge. They have the very kind of information that you need to understand the present system.

Remember: You can't absorb information while *you* are talking.

7. A POLICY ON JOB ELIMINATION

More than a generation ago, organizations started to develop wise policies that they applied to systems survey work. The policy covered systems improvement and any resulting job elimination. If working people think of you as being a job eliminator (or as a "hatchet" man or woman) you cannot expect them to welcome you.

Yes, it *is* sometimes necessary to eliminate useless jobs or other forms of waste. And we don't suggest that you compromise here.

Look at it this way. If there is waste, is it not because management has failed to order a systems survey for so long that much waste has crept in? Then who is responsible for such waste? The employee or management? Obviously it is management. Therefore management should recognize its responsibility for waste. Wise managements do.

They recognize that if a man (or woman) is to do systems survey work, he would be severely handicapped if the people involved feared that they would lose their jobs. Most organizations in the United States and Canada now have definite policies on this delicate subject, usually stated something like this:

In making improvements on systems or on individual jobs, no employee need be concerned about the loss of his job or about any reduction in his pay or his job status as a result of those improvements.

To the worker the loss of a job is a personal disaster. It can have repercussions in his marital status and in his family and social life. Without adequate income he suffers a severe economic dislocation. Sometimes jobs must be eliminated and layoffs must take place . . . for economic reasons. Organizations cannot carry people when there is no work for them.

Companies and organizations that have a policy similar to the one quoted sometimes make a layoff *before* conducting a survey. In most cases, particularly in a growth period, normal turnover takes care of a displaced employee, or the person can be retrained to fill a new position.

8. PREPARING YOURSELF FOR THE INTERVIEW

Henri Fayol, the great French philosopher and practitioner of management, had this advice for the engineers that he brought into his company as manager-trainees:

Maintain toward workers a polite and kindly attitude: Set out to study their behavior, character, abilities, work and even their personal interests.

Remember that intelligent men are to be found in every walk of life. Bring suspension of judgment and a sense of proportion to bear upon your assessment of things and of the people around you.

To use criticism with the idea of contributing to improvement is good, but criticisms of any other kind are an act of levity or malevolence.

Fayol gave that advice in 1905. Yet it's just as useful and applicable today as it was at the turn of the century.

9. SELECTING PEOPLE TO INTERVIEW

How many actors did you discover as you combed through the documents? That's the number of people you should interview. Each one has a different function, does a different job. Of course if the same function is being handled by 8 or 10 people (such as the buyers in the purchasing department) you may not have time to talk to all of them. But you will talk to at least one such person. Choose the natural leader (or the senior person) in that activity. If you don't know who this person is, the supervisor can tell you.

Reminder: If you are going to talk to workers in a department, you must first clear this step with their supervisor. It is normal to spend a little time with the supervisor before talking to his workers.

Even though supervisors direct the people who do the work, sometimes they are not up to date on all the details. That's why you must talk to the people who actually do the work.

Are there a number of people to interview within one department? Have the supervisor announce your coming. You might prepare a suggested memo for the supervisor to send out. Ask him if he'll sign it and send it to his people. This will help to smooth the way for you.

10. PREPARING THE PERSON TO BE INTERVIEWED

If the employee doesn't work for you, he needs a word from his own boss. Who are you? Why are you coming in to talk to him?

Are you a line manager? If you're making the study in your own department, tell your employees why you are making the study. Hold a five-minute meeting. Explain that you will be talking to certain people. Tell all your people the purpose of the study.

If your organization does have a policy on preservation of an employee's pay or job status, remind them of this. (If there is no such policy, your organization should develop one.)

What should you know about the person that you're going to talk to? If he works for you, you may think you know him, but why not review his records now? What are his hobbies? What is his education? Has he taken any job-related classes in the last year? How long has he been with the organization? What kind of progress has he been making over the years? What is his job title? What tasks does he perform in *this* system? (One worker may be involved in three or four different systems.)

Will that person need to do some research (homework) before you talk to him? Should he gather some information? Statistics? Examples of troublesome transactions? Tell him so by telephone, by memo, or face to face.

You know the routine of the system. You know generally what the individual does at this processing point. Therefore you can construct two or three specific questions to use during the interview.

Structure those questions so that the person cannot answer "yes" or "no." *Don't* say, "Does this order still come to you directly from the salesman?" *Do* say, "When this order from the salesman reaches you, how do you prepare it for the data entry operation to the computer?"

If the order doesn't come from the salesman any longer, you'll find out now.

Here's an example of a question that can be answered with a yes or a no. "I understand copy number two of this forms set comes to you from the billing department. Is that right?" Such a question may draw a "yes" or "no" response.

Rephrase it. You already know that the copy comes from the billing department; the documents told you this. So ask: "When copy two of this forms set comes to you from the billing department, to whom does it come first? What does she do with it? What happens to it after she has added that information?"

11. STARTING THE INTERVIEW

Take a few minutes to break the ice. Discuss some subject of mutual interest
. . . a hobby such as golf, growing roses, football, skiing, piloting airplanes,
collecting stamps. *Don't talk about you.* Talk about HIM! You do this by simply asking questions, not by giving answers. You may have had some delight-
ful experiences that you want to tell him about, but restrain yourself.

The purpose of the few minutes of light talk is to establish a relaxed, pleasant relationship with the person. Five minutes is ample.

As you talk to a worker, place in front of him the two key systems documents, your grid chart and a filled-out copy of the major action form. As noted
earlier, it is important to turn them around on the desk so that *he* sees them and
can read them. After you explain briefly why you are making the study, point
out the individual's work column, his position on the chart. Then ask one of
your preplanned questions.

Ask yourself, "Can this person fill in a gap for me? Can he give me an answer that I couldn't find in the documents?" If so, your first questions can be
about that gap. *"How* does this order go from here to there? *What* do you do
with it when it comes in? *How* do you do that?"

Use your grid chart and action form as you interview, to focus the person's
attention on the work sequence.

You're not giving answers. You're *asking* questions. If what this person does was fairly clear from your reading of the documents, you'll want to know if the information in those documents is up to date. Verify the facts you obtained from such documents. Is this how the person now does it?

Each time that you approach a person to interview him, ask:

1. Can this person fill in a gap, provide a link that seems to be missing, or fill in a hole for me?
2. Can this person verify a fact that I gleaned from the documents?

Invite the man to talk about his views of the present system . . . what is good about it . . . what is bad about it . . . what works well . . . and what does not work so well.

Remember: If someone gives you an idea on what should be done, write it down. Put the person's name on it. Date it. Later, if you use that idea in the new system, give him credit for it.

12. INTERVIEWING SEQUENCE?
FOLLOW THE CHANNEL

Interview the people in the same sequence they follow to do their work in the system's channel. Talk first to the person who originates the transaction, who works at the trigger point. Talk last to the person who is at the other end of the channel, where the teamwork activity leads to the final result.

Follow the channel, and your work will go easier. As you pick up information, printed forms, and other examples, give them the same numbers you gave the work stations on your grid chart.

If you are interviewing a clerk at processing point 7, all forms, all notes you may take, any ideas for credits to the suggestor, all can go by the numbers. Thus all details relating to what happens at the seventh work point in the channel can be placed in one folder labeled "Station 7—Order Processing Clerk."

13. EMPATHY

What is the other person thinking as you talk to him or to her? Are you really welcome? At first, possibly not. Working against you may be some of the worker's not so pleasant experiences of the past. Such events often cause his thoughts to flow as follows:

Who is this fellow? Is he an efficiency expert?
What's he up to?
Is he spying on me?
Is a big cut coming in our staff?
Why is he asking all these questions?
What will he do with this information?
Will his report go to my boss?
Will anything that he is doing really have value?
Does he think I'm not able to do my job?

What is a fact? As you talk to people you will be making notes. You'll be acquiring information you couldn't find by merely reading documents. But you will also get new facts and new information that did not appear on the documents.

Here are some of the things you are going to want to know as you talk to an operator:

1. How does the work reach the worker?
2. What is the form of the work? (A printed form?)
3. How many people are doing the same type of work?
4. How long does it take to handle a transaction as far as this station is concerned?
5. Exactly what is the person doing to the transaction at this point? (You're looking for his "contribution.")

From your study of sciences you may recall that a fact is defined as follows:

[a] close agreement on something that exists and is real, and is derived from a series of observations, any one of which can be verified at any time.

The information that you will get from your people can fall into four classifications:

☐ 1. Information that is not a fact
☐ 2. Information that is partially factual
☐ 3. Information that has no bearing on your study
☐ 4. Information that is highly significant

Think about each "fact." Is it really a fact? It can be embarrassing to you if you accept a bit of erroneous information on face value.

When you get to the proposal stage of your study, it's entirely possible that a sharp executive will test you on a minor point, on some fact (that he knows), to see how accurate your study has been.

Reminder: As the details that you have gathered, including those from the interviews, begin to pile up, raise your head. Look up high. Ask again, "What is the real objective of this system?" Regain your perspective.

14. STAY ON THE MAIN LINE

As you move through the systems channel, you know that there is a main channel and side channels . . . eddies, tributaries, some coming in and some going off from the principal channel. As you move from one work process station to another, ask:

Am I still on the main line?

Stay on the main line; learn to recognize when you've been switched off onto a sidetrack.

By staying alert you won't get switched off onto a side channel without knowing it. If there is a related systems cycle, one that comes into or goes off from yours, certainly you want to know that. When you redesign the system, most of these subsystems also must be considered.

It is easy to go off on a tangent, then go around and around and not get back on the main line at all . . . if you aren't alert.

15. TRANSACTIONAL ANALYSIS

The interview is an example of a *personal* transaction. Notice that we have been using the term *transaction* to indicate a unit of business that flows through the system. Both types are transactions, but one is routine (the systems transaction) and the other is personal (nonroutine).

The most productive interviews are on what Dr. Thomas Harris (in *I'm OK—You're OK* *) calls the "adult level." On that level both you and the interviewee talk calmly and constructively. There is no feeling that you are on the offensive (attacking him) or that the other person is on the defensive. You are two mature people. You are equal partners in the task of making a system work better.

For a full explanation of the adult aspect of our personalities, read Harris' book. It will open your eyes as to the three facets of our personalities: (1) parent, (2) child, and (3) adult. Both you and the person you are interviewing possess those three personality aspects.

From a systems viewpoint here are examples of these different personality aspects brought out by the words the person speaks:

1. Response from a person's "parent" aspect (finger shaking): You shouldn't do it that way.
2. Response from a person's "child" aspect (pettish): Well, I just like to do it this way.
3. Response from the adult aspect of a person (calmly and patiently): Do you think that this idea would work if the orders arrived as late as 9:00 a.m.?

As interviewer you must keep the adult aspect of your personality in full charge at all times. Your mature approach tends to bring out the "adult" in the person you are talking to.

* Avon Publishing, 1973.

An effective interview is impossible if the parent (critical) or child (pouting, whiny, or subservient) aspects of either person are in the ascendancy.

Sometimes you may recognize that the individual you are talking to is not being adult. He may be fearful, defensive, evasive, or emotionally upset. If you recognize this, gently break off the interview. Tell him you'd like to see him later. Then leave.

16. WHAT IS NOW—NOT WHAT SHOULD BE!

As you talk to a person, keep reminding yourself that you are not yet redesigning the system. You are not actively seeking to get ideas on what the new system *should* be. Keep asking questions that will tell you *more about the present system!* And you are to ask questions . . . not to give answers.

People will be stimulated by your questions. Many will jump to a conclusion about what should be done. Accept these ideas, but make no comment. Thank the person. Point out that the idea "will be considered."

At this stage, you're still working to achieve a clear picture of the present system. If *you* jump to a conclusion about what should be done too soon, you may hurt the quality of the new system you design later. Restrain yourself. You will start the redesign work only after you have all the facts and after you have analyzed those facts.

Do not criticize. Do not indicate even by a raised eyebrow that you are critical of a person or of what he is doing. If the person you are talking to criticizes someone else, neither agree nor disagree. Just make a note of what he says. It may be a symptom. Be pleasant. Be noncommittal.

You can courteously and consistently keep asking questions . . . pertinent questions. Keep focusing the worker's attention on the chart or on the form that you have placed in front of him.

17. GET MORE DOCUMENTS

Ask. Only if you ask, will you receive more documents. Does the worker have any instruction sheets? Does he have an organization chart? Does he have some special forms he uses? Logs? Lists? Ask for copies. Are there any work output standards? Any work measurements, such as how many orders should be processed by one person in an eight-hour day?

Does he have any charts on the "peaks and valleys" of the work? Many persons who are working in the system have answers to such questions, answers you can get only here . . . out on the "working floor."

It is particularly important that you get any copies of reports, records, or action forms that you have not yet seen. Ask for filled-out copies. Get a number of samples. If the interviewee can't let you have the originals, can you go to the office copier and make duplicates?

18. HANDLING OBSTACLES IN THE INTERVIEW

Sometimes people play games with you. They try to see if they can divert you to some other type of conversation. Or they talk so much that they go way beyond the cycle of the system that you are studying. Or they go deeply into sidetrack problems.

When the interview is interrupted, consider how you'll get the person back on the track. Don't tune in on the interruption.

Your chart is your guide. By glancing at it you can recognize when the conversation is going far afield. Bring it back. Say, "Mr. Williams, may we get back to my other question, the one covering _____?"

During the interview you will also experience interruptions. The phone will ring, or a co-worker will come in with something that is "hot." Each time there is an interruption, the person's train of thought will be broken. His mind will switch off the track that you and he have been following together.

When the interruption is over, bring your man (or woman) back onto the track. The person may not remember exactly where the two of you stopped. He has been distracted by other information, probably relating to a subject that isn't at all germane to your interview.

Don't listen in on the interruption. Concentrate on what you have been doing. Make a note of where you stood on the "interview path." Mentally review what you have already covered. Read the next structured question you wanted to ask. As soon as the interruption is over, remind the man of what you had been discussing:

Mr. Williams, when the phone rang we were discussing the question of the number of transactions that seem to peak up on Mondays and on the first of the month . . .

19. SHOULD YOU TAKE NOTES?

Yes. Tell the person that you are going to be making some notes on the information he gives you. If you think it's necessary (to make him feel secure), you can say, "After I get these notes rewritten and perhaps typed, would you like to look at them to be sure that the information is accurate?"

Identify each set of notes. Place a number in the upper right corner of the paper. Use the work sequence number that you put on your grid chart. As you pick up any other information such as instructions, forms, job outlines, job descriptions, reports, special memo copies, and so on, number those. Again use your grid chart processing point number.

Have you collected quite a bundle of notes? If your notes amount to more than two or three pages and you also have picked up five or six other exhibits, make a file folder to hold all the information related to this processing point. Number and title the folder, like this:

Work Station 17—PROOFING

20. HOW LONG?

Keep your interview short. Limit it to about 20 minutes. It's better to conduct several short interviews over a period of days than it is to have one long one.

Sometimes the circumstances are such that you will not get all the information that you need . . . and you will have to come back. So always leave the door open by saying to the person:

Mr. Williams, I think I have all the information I need here to see how the present system is working. However, if I find that I do need more, I will give you a call or arrange to come back.

21. ORDERLY RESEARCH

When you get back to your desk, review your notes quickly. If you have a typing facility, dictate your notes.

If you have identified 15 different processing points in the system (work stations between the start of the cycle and its end), make up 15 file folders. Number each with the process station number. This technique helps to keep your information in good order and in logical systems sequence. All pertinent detail relating to the work that goes on at each processing station can go into one folder.

Please keep in mind that later, as you redesign the system, you will talk again to the same people. Then you will stress what *should* be done in the new system, rather than what is happening in the present system.

By now you have gathered most of the facts you're going to need. So you move on to the next signpost on your "classic path" to systems improvement. It is the analysis stage.

CHAPTER 8

ANALYSIS AND MEDITATION

When you have gathered most of the facts relating to the present system (you'll never get them all), you are ready to go to the next stage on your classic route to systems improvement . . . analysis. After you have analyzed the facts that pertain to the present system, you will be ready to design a better system.

1. WHERE ARE YOU NOW ON CLASSIC PATH?

You are now at signpost 6. Analysis is the stage between fact gathering and design. The term *analysis* refers to the process of taking apart and studying each element. It also indicates a study of the relationships of the different elements.

So design (or more accurately, redesign) is the opposite of analysis. In analysis you take apart; in redesign you put together or synthesize.

☞ The excellence of your final design depends on the *quality* of your previous steps!

So the quality of analysis is important. Yet analysis, being a mental process, isn't easy to describe. Furthermore, people use different styles for their individual analysis processes. The best we can do here is describe the process we have used. We can also report that most of our students have found the guidance to be of real help in developing their analysis techniques.

2. USE THE TRANSACTION AS A PIVOT

Pivot your analysis around the transaction. It is the common denominator of the system. The transaction, represented by a cluster of data items, is the vehicle that moves through the systems channel. You'll need to know quite a bit about the transactions that flow through your system's channel. Typical transactions include a sale, a claim, a collection, a shipment, and a payment.

Did you identify the key action form—the form carrying the data and reflecting the transaction? How about the connections with the system's memory? How many records do people keep that reflect the transactions?

Who posts or updates the memories as the transactions move through? A clerk? A computer? How many transactions are handled in a specific period of time, such as one month?

What is the span of time needed for the transaction to make the trip through the systems channel—on an average? Three days? Four hours? Two weeks? This is a time measurement of the span of time required to complete the *average* transaction.

Perhaps the transaction's trigger is a sales order. This is an action form. Examine it carefully. The data on it represents the transaction. If it comes in on Monday morning (in the 8 a.m. mail), your question could be: "When will the goods ordered be out of our shop and on the way to our customer?" The span time is always in calendar time. It may be five days, three days . . . it could be three weeks. But do know what it is.

Notice we said "on an average." Do some transactions take longer than the average? If the average is five days, do some transactions take twice that long? If 1000 transactions go through in a week (200 per day, average) how many of the 1000 go through in the normal (average) span of time? Do any go through *faster* than the average? (You will wonder why.) Do some go through in a time much longer than the average? (You'll also want to know why.)

Give close attention to the action form. It represents a transaction. Know the purpose of every data item.

3.   USE AN ANALYSIS CHECKLIST

In addition to your knowledge of the transaction, you should have information about other items relating to the system, including:

1. The physical distances that the transaction flows . . . in feet, meters, or miles.
2. The exact physical route of the flow channel (perhaps through several departments).
3. How much of the time (during the in-the-house span of time) is the transaction being *worked* on? How much of the time is it *waiting?* How much of the time is it being *moved* from one work station to another?
4. What is the quality situation? How many errors? The percentage? How are they corrected? What causes such errors? What safeguards exist to catch errors before the transaction enters the system? Do some people cover up errors?
5. Supervisory control. If something doesn't go right, such as a log jam of

transactions in the channel, who moves in and breaks the jam and gets the transactions flowing again?

6. Discipline on meeting schedules. If orders are bogging down and getting through later and later, who moves in on this situation?

7. Other communications. Are there communications that go on in addition to the moving of the key form (which reflects the transaction)? Any personal contacts between people at work stations? Phoning? Special forms? Memos sent between these people? Personal visits?

8. Transcriptions. How many times is the data copied from the action form *to* records or to other forms? Or *from* other forms or records to the action form?

9. What about the exercise of authority? Who signs? Who approves? Is there some "rubber stamping"?

10. What special equipment is used? Conveyor belts, special files, electric trucks, pneumatic tube systems . . . internal mail systems?

11. Does the computer do some of the systems work or most of it? Exactly what functions does it perform? Store data? Do arithmetic? Compare balances? Provide for immediate access to the file? Print out summaries? Display data on a cathode ray tube (CRT)?

12. Any terminals in use? Where located? Who uses? Is data transmission two-way?

13. Records (systems memories). Whether on cards or disks, how many records must be updated every time a transaction flows through the channel. Who or what does the updating?

14. Reports (the systems kind). Who gets them? What do they do with them? How often issued? Value? Designed for reader's convenience?

4. PREPARING FOR ANALYSIS

Our normal, rigid thinking is out. To bubble up useful ideas, your mind must be flexible . . . resilient beyond the normal. As you analyze the facts gathered in your study, don't take anything for granted. Challenge even the most basic assumptions. Two questions (what? and why?) are the analyst's most useful pry-up and fit-together tools.

You are working on a giant jigsaw puzzle. How do you fit the pieces together? What pieces connect to what other pieces?

Normally we view our environment from an individual frame of reference. This frame is like a window in a wall, a single view that is always restricted. We don't always realize this, but it is so.

Your objective now is to mentally break out the whole wall . . . or go to another, a bigger window. You can do this by asking challenging questions. For example, when you are considering the activity at one work station, you can ask:

1. Why do we do this work *here?*
2. Why should we do this work *first?*
3. Why don't we do it *last?*
4. What would happen if we *didn't do* it at all?
5. What would happen if we did it *somewhere else?*
6. Why does *this person* do it?
7. What would happen if *someone else* did it?
8. Can someone *outside* the organization do it?

Notice the words "what" and "why." Challenging questions can help you smash your present frame of reference. Avoid being a prisoner of your own thought patterns. You could ask other questions, such as these:

1. What would happen if we turned this over?
2. What would happen if we did this backward?
3. What would happen if we moved this operation to a different place?

As the answers come, new ideas will be generated. Spin these ideas around in your head. Look at the problem from the back. Then work toward the front. Or come at the problem from the middle. Go first to the left and then to the right. Crawl under. Crawl over. Break into the middle of the sequence. Look both ways.

To be effective at analysis you must climb out of your personal mental ruts. Ever notice how routine your trip to the office is? You drive along the same street or highway, you pass certain stop lights and many familiar scenes. Do you *really* see these details each morning? You probably don't.

We all live with mental blinders on our eyes. Until we learn how to shake off those blinders, we can't really do a good job of analyzing.

A mental rut is not a suitable site for developing a useful new idea.

5. LOOK AT YOUR PICTURE OF THE SYSTEM

You took a grid flow chart with you when you interviewed people during the study. As you received up-to-date information about the system, you probably revised the chart.

Keep that revised grid chart in front of you now. It will help you maintain your perspective on the entire system. Then, when you're considering a single facet (such as one item of data that goes on one specific record), you can see how the one data item fits into the system.

One systems analyst keeps his perspective on the entire system by using two 4×8 foot boards fastened to his wall. This gives him a chart 4 feet high and 16 feet long. He gets the actual forms used in the system and pins them on the board. Then he uses wide, colored tape to indicate the flow across the board. This "life-size" grid chart helps him to see exactly where he is in the entire pattern at any stage.

So that he can identify these forms from a distance (10 or 12 feet), he uses a bold black ink pen and hand letters the title on the face of each form such as: Invoice, Bill of Lading, Packing Slip, Inspection Notice, Disk File, Shipping Order, Schedule. He letters the titles 1 inch high so that people helping him study the system can identify each form without having to go up to the board.

6. CLASSIFY

Your grid chart gives you an overview of the system. It reveals the entire channel, from the trigger to the result. You know each work station located along that channel. You know what people do at each station.

Now you are in the process of taking the entire system apart . . . identifying elements that you can sort out. One of the more powerful techniques of analysis is classification. Look for related classes of the system's parts.

Consider the data function in the system. How many action forms are used? How many records? How many reports? How many nonofficial (bootleg) forms?

Exactly what people skills are required? How many people provide stenographic skills? Accounting skills? Credit skills? Sales skills? Inspection skills? The total man-hours used to complete each transaction?

Sort and classify by office work actions. How many people *check* information? How many *approve?* How many *transcribe* information from one form to another?

As you're doing this detailed work (mentally breaking the system into its parts), don't lose your perspective. Put the grid chart on the wall in front of you, and look at it. The grid chart provides the overview of the system and helps you see the relationships between the various elements that you are now sorting and classifying.

7. VERIFY THE FACTS

You can't verify every fact you have gathered, but be careful that the *key* facts are accurate. You know, now, what information is most significant.

What facts are crucial? The number of transactions is one crucial fact. Are you sure of the number? Do you accept Mr. Jones' word as accurate when he says, "On an average we handle 1000 of these order transactions each week."

You can verify Mr. Jones' "fact" by checking at the stationery stockroom. Ask the clerk to look up his record. The record may show that Mr. Jones withdrew only 31,000 of those forms last year.

Mr. Jones told you "1000 a week." A thousand a week is 52,000 a year. Yet the withdrawals indicate only 31,000. Here you find an apparent discrepancy. What caused it? Is there a supply of forms out in Mr. Jones' stationery cabinet? Or is Mr. Jones' figure of a thousand a week in error?

Of course you can't check every fact. You would not have time. But your knowledge of what is *significant* and what is *not* significant will now come into play.

Do check all the significant facts. You're not balancing to the penny. You just need reasonable accuracy. If one source says 52,000 action forms and another says 53,000, you may consider these answers to be reasonably in agreement.

8. IDENTIFY THE EXCEPTIONAL
TRANSACTIONS

Are there some transactions that cannot be handled well on a routine basis? If so, do people try to handle them routinely anyway?

If 10% of the transactions are really variations and do not go through the channel smoothly (tend to bottleneck the systems channel), what is the best way to handle them? Further classify the 10%. Some of the variations will be of one type, others of another type. And there will be one or two exceptional transactions that have no companion variations. They are unique. Should they even be in the system? (Remember that a system is a plan for handling work on a routine, low-cost basis.) If such "oddballs" should be handled individually, how does the operator identify them? Tell her, and establish a procedure that allows the operator to flip them out of the system and hand them to a qualified individual for personal (not routine) handling.

If the systems channel becomes choked with too many transactions or too many exceptions, the transactions will be handled poorly and slowly.

No one can plan for a rare variation or exception, such as one in 5000. It just isn't worthwhile to set up a system that will handle that one exceptional transaction. Plan to take such a transaction out of the system. Help the operator identify it as a difficult transaction. Then let the proper person decide how to handle it.

9. MEDITATE: USE POWERFUL SUBCONSCIOUS

Meditation is signpost 7 on the classic path to systems improvement. About 99% of our waking day we are governed or driven by our conscious mind . . . or by our emotions. Perhaps not since your school days have you tried to reach into your elusive but powerful subconscious mind.

But now *try* to reach it. You must have its help.

You have numerous factual inputs gathered from your survey. Read and review your notes. Examine the forms, records, and reports. Feed thoughts based on your hoard of facts into your common, everyday (conscious) mind. Then try to fold them back, tuck them up into your important mind . . . THE SUBCONSCIOUS.

To use your subconscious mind you must know its characteristics, then work in harmony with them. You can't force the subconscious mind. It won't take orders. You can't bully it.

If you know its characteristics, you'll know how to persuade it to give you a hand in developing your new system. Consider:

1. Your subconscious cannot work in a vacuum. You must feed it information. (Read and reread the facts you've gathered.)
2. It works best if you are relaxed, patient, and quiet.
3. Your subconscious will accept your help. Feed it the significant bits of information, rather than a big volume of unimportant facts.
4. Information alone won't do it. Feed it stimulating information . . . facts that spark further thinking.
5. You can't command your subconscious to give you answers. You've got to coax it.
6. You'll help your subconscious immensely if you implant in it the TRUE WORK PURPOSE of the system you're studying.
7. Your subconscious mind may pour out ideas and thoughts at any time. Be ready to capture them. Jot them down quickly.

Use your powerful subconscious mind. It will help design a better system.

8. Be quiet. Relax. If you engage in intense physical activity, you'll suppress the activities of your subconscious mind.
9. The subconscious can work on several problems at one time.

Slow down now. Your subconscious will be useless if you are in a hurry. You only hamper it by your anxiety, emotionalism, or worry. Your subconscious will not accept deadlines. You can induce it to work for you only by the gentlest of coddling.

10.   CAN YOU USE A THINKING ROOM?

It's hard to get a quality result if you have to think in an open area with distractions, noise, and many people around. The quality of your thinking will be improved if you retreat to a room where you can be by yourself. This is a "thinking room." You should keep it for a number of days. If the survey job is a really big one, you'll need the room for a number of weeks. Consider: perhaps your own office can serve as a thinking room.

1. Is it well ventilated?
2. Well lighted?

3. Quiet?
4. Comfortable?

The analyst may be able to turn on his creative powers in an area with typewriters clattering, people talking, phones ringing, and interruptions. But a man will do a better job if he can work in reasonable quiet. Analysis is a form of thinking in depth, and the physical environment around the analyst can *contribute* to his thinking process or *detract* from it.

If you are going to design a powerful, useful, and straightforward system, the very best thinking will be none too good.

It's important to remember that when you design a new system, you are in the process of making a major decision that ranks in importance with the 15 or 20 most significant decisions that your management will make during the year. Once you've made that decision and your management has accepted it, the resulting system will be with you and your organization, for better or worse, for years. It could be, over the years, a multimillion dollar decision.

The new system may require that you spend money to make changes, perhaps to purchase new computers, new peripheral gear, or other equipment. You are therefore committing your organization, on a financial operational basis, to use the plan that you devise. And the system cannot be any better than your thinking. So think.

That's why a thinking room is so important. The environment that facilitates inductive thinking can contribute to your penetrating analysis.

11. HOW MANY ELEMENTS?

How many parts of the system have you been able to identify: Some are physical items. Here is a checklist that may help you. Any given system may have more items, but you will usually be able to identify these.

1. People and their skills
2. Supervisors and controls
3. Data (information)
4. Machines (from pencils to computers)
5. Procedures
6. Policies
7. Job outlines and instructions
8. Action forms
9. Reports
10. Man-hours
11. Materials
12. Supplies
13. Layout of the floor
14. Work stations (or desks)
15. Distances between work stations and total distance
16. Transportation

17. Files
18. Exceptions
19. Variations
20. Quality checks
21. Error correction
22. Computer programs
23. Physical environment (air, heat, etc.)
24. Subsystems
    a. in-flowing
    b. out-flowing
25. The origin of the action
26. The result (end of the action
27. Audit points in the system
28. The channel
29. The cycle's extent
30. Records
31. Software
32. Connecting systems
    a. before this *trigger*
    b. after this *result*

Consider item 1, *people and their skills*. One person at one work station may use four or five distinct skills. A system may use 100 or more skills.

12.   KNOW THE CAST OF CHARACTERS

Systems improvement work can be dull business if you don't approach it in the right way and with the right attitude. Think of the activity . . . of people taking actions in the systems channel . . . as an interesting human drama. The entire organization is a big stage, and human actors are playing different roles. These roles have to do with work.

The most interesting elements of the system are the people who use that system. Study and appreciate them.

Give special attention to the people who do the work *in* the system. Know them. Respect them. They represent the spirit and the life of the system. Operating people push the transaction along. They contribute to its completion. Supervisors may play an indirect role . . . that of control. Others such as staff people, auditors, or accountants, may also play subsidiary roles in the systems activity.

As you set aside the elements of the system, give special attention to the people. What are their job titles? What do they do as the work relates TO the system? Write the exact job title in this manner:

Work station No. 5. Order Processing Clerk (Susie Hamilton)

Next write (briefly) what she does in the system, using the same numbers you used on the grid chart. Continue to do this for each person at each station.

13.   IDEATION

Now you're coming close to the design step. Ideas on better ways will begin to come—if you have done a thorough job of analysis.

No one knows quite how the subconscious mind works, but we know that it *does* work.

Ideas on what one facet of the new system should be (the output of your subconscious mind) may come to you at any time. You may be in church, traveling in your car, at the office, or at a party. You may be at the theater. Carry a pencil and paper with you at all times.

After a time of gestation, ideas about what the new system should be will flutter out of your mind. They won't necessarily flutter out during working hours. They may come to you at any time. Be prepared to catch them. When the idea comes, write it down. You may be tempted to say, "Oh, I'll write that down later. I'll remember it."

 You won't remember it. At least you won't remember it with all its potency. You might lose the idea completely. And you can't afford to lose a good idea. You worked hard to get it. Capture it now by writing it down.

Meditation is individual action. So is ideation. In the process called ideation, you sit at your desk and look up at the chart and at the system's objective. Then you look down at some of the facts you have on your desk.

You'll be asking questions like, "Will this idea overcome the problems we encountered in this system?" "How can we make this system the best ever?" "How can we go from the trigger to the result quickly, easily, and cheaply?"

What you're trying to do now is come up with ideas that are potentially a part of the new design . . . but you don't want such ideas to get set in cement . . . not just yet. They must not become rigid at this point.

14. BRAINSTORM

After a period of ideation, the next phase of your analysis work is to brainstorm. This means that you will talk to other people who are involved in the system. You'll also talk to others who have advised you—consultants, accountants, auditors, and so on. You will try out some of your ideas on them. Brainstorming is an especially stimulating activity. Use the ideas you generated by ideation to prime other people's mental pumps.

Avoid mental cement. Keep your mind flexible. Ask people questions, such as: "In your case, how do you think *this* would work when we revise the system?" Let them comment on one specific idea.

If some of the ideas you picked up from your original interviewing are a part of your list of ideas, by all means go to the contributors of those ideas. Explore each idea again with the person who suggested it.

Before you see other people, you may want to rough out a new grid chart, showing the path you think the new system should take. Take this revised chart with you as you brainstorm. This isn't yet your final grid chart—the one that will show your new system in all its glory.

Perhaps three or four of the people can get together to brainstorm for 30 minutes or an hour. Use your thinking room. Give each person a copy of this revised chart. Discuss the various "good ideas." Such discussions are very stimulating. Ideas will flow.

Keep all ideas for redesign entirely flexible. You developed a new chart, and so on, and are going a little ahead of the other people simply because the others need a spring board for their thinking. They, like you, cannot think in a vacuum. So what you are doing is offering them trial balloons.

When you talk to the people, you wonder if the new ideas make sense, if the new plan that is forming in your mind is valid. Can the ideas stand up under the scrutiny of the people who will use them? Ask them.

A system can't be any better than the thinking that goes into it. Use brain-storming as a design tool.

15. TEST YOUR IDEAS

Carry on with the participation process. At this stage the people are likely to react quickly to any specifics. In creative work many good ideas bubble up . . . but others that are *not* good also surface. Sometimes an idea seems quite good to the analyst, but when he gets the viewpoint of the practical people he realizes that his idea is impractical.

What we are considering now are the healthy "pin pricks" that will keep you from making major blunders as you redesign.

Getting many pats on the back? Do you hear: "Great idea! That's fine!" Be careful if you get too many compliments. Something is probably wrong. If people won't take a healthy crack at what you offer, they are afraid of you, don't want to commit themselves, or don't care.

Go out of your way to talk to a good thinker who will be objective about what should be done. During the survey you probably ran across a man or woman who wouldn't pull any punches. Such a person can give you the tough, blunt responses that you need and should seek.

Do not take your ideas to a loyal friend who will approve almost anything you do.

Do not be thin-skinned about these pin pricks. They are healthy. Now is the time to find out that an idea won't work . . . or to discover that the people in the system *think* that it won't work, which is almost the same thing.

If you try to force a new idea down people's throats and they are convinced that it will not work . . . it won't.

You alone could do all the analysis work we have been discussing. As soon as you have some definite ideas, however, you should always get back to the people who will run the system. The "process of participation" goes on at this stage, for two reasons.

1. You can check your ideas to be sure they are down to earth and that they will fit into the new system.
2. You continue with the important job of keeping people informed and letting them be in on things as the new system develops. You are a part of the team and so are they!

Furthermore you will be stimulated by the responses you get. You will continue to pick up some facts . . . information you didn't think you would need. The fact-gathering process that you concentrated on earlier will go on until the new system is actually installed.

Observation: Please recognize that there is no sharp dividing line between the various steps on the classic route to systems improvement. One step merges into the other. Often you'll go back and do some work you thought you had covered in a previous step. *Example:* While you are redesigning, you may do some analysis or meditation or fact gathering.

Even during the stage of checking ideas with other people, you may find that something you had accepted as fact now appears to be questionable. Someone may say, "Well, I just don't think we handled that many transactions last year. I think it was more like half of that."

At each step on the classic path, you do try to concentrate on one type of activity to the exclusion of others. One time you are gathering facts from documents, the next from people, and next you're analyzing all those facts. Even at the pin-prick stage, or in preliminary testing, you concentrate on getting people reactions. But some or any of those activities can take place all along the path.

When you think you have done enough in the way of analyzing, you are ready to consider the following questions:

What should the new system be like? How will it overcome the problem encountered in the present one?

CHAPTER 9

DESIGNING THE NEW SYSTEM

You are at signpost 8 on the classic path. This is the synthesis (rebuilding stage) of your systems improvement work. By now you probably know that system better than anyone else in the organization.

You may not be familiar with all the details that each worker knows about *his* individual job, but you know what work each man, each woman, and each machine in the system does. You know how each individual effort contributes to the forward progress of the transaction as it flows through the system's channel. You know how the parts fit into the whole picture.

You have a vision of that channel always before you. Now you are ready to design a new system (actually to redesign the present one). You are convinced that a new system will serve better than the present one. And above all it must eliminate the condition that is causing trouble in the current system.

1. WHAT IS A "BETTER" SYSTEM?

Naturally you want your new system to do a great job . . . to be a much better system than the present one. "Better" could mean:

1. *Faster.* A shorter span of time between trigger and result.
2. *Less expensive.* If you costed the present system and found that it averaged $8 per transaction, will the new cost per transaction be $6? $7? $5?
3. *Better service.* Will customers, patrons, or clients feel better about your results?
4. *More control.* Will supervisors be in a better position to keep the action on the track?
5. Will *fewer man-hours* be used?
6. Will the people need *less equipment?*
7. Use *less floor space?*
8. Generate *less paper* and *fewer records?*
9. Require *fewer processing points* along the channel?
10. Will there be *easier* or *pleasanter* work for people in the system?
11. Will the system generate *fewer errors?* It costs about 10 times as much to correct a mistake as it does to avoid the error.

During the analysis and meditation stage, ideas tumbled out. When they did, you captured them by writing them down. You encountered an immense number of details. Now you may feel that you are wandering through a confusing labyrinth of paths and bypaths.

2. LOOK AT THE SYSTEM'S OBJECTIVE AGAIN

You are going to deal with myriads of details as you design the new system. Don't get bogged down mentally! How do you avoid that?

In the design phase your guiding star is the *new* system's objective. Get a fix on it. Write it out, specifically. Then keep your eye on it at all times.

During your study of the present system, you wrote down the objective of that system. And you noted the essential subobjectives. Do you now feel, from what you've learned, that the objective of the new system will be the same? Modified? Substantially different? Completely different? How about each of the subobjectives? Should your new system serve the same subobjectives? Drop some? Add some?

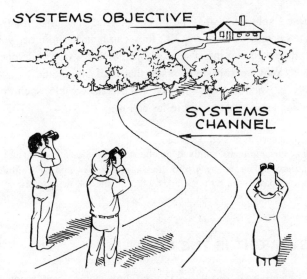

SYSTEMS OBJECTIVE

SYSTEMS CHANNEL

As you redesign the system, focus on the objective.

Validate each subobjective by asking hard questions like, "Why do we need to reach that subobjective?" "What will happen if we don't reach it?" "Can this entire system be abolished?" "If not, can someone else do the work and get the result *for* us?" "Why should *we* do it?"

Such questions shake some people up. Yet as the analyst you should ask them. If you're studying the shipping system, you may simply state that the work objective is "to ship goods."

That shipping objective sounds like a result that must be achieved, doesn't it? But challenge it. Ask:

- ☐ Why should we ship the goods?
- ☐ Should we get our own trucks?
- ☐ Why couldn't our customers come here and pick up their goods?
- ☐ Why couldn't we set up a serve-yourself deal?
- ☐ Are we shipping too far . . . or too much?
- ☐ Should we have warehouses closer to our customers?
- ☐ Could a shipping service do the job for us?
- ☐ Can we cut down the quantity of shipment by pooling them?
- ☐ Could we get the customers to order in larger quantities?
- ☐ Or order more of different articles?
- ☐ Can several customers in the same city pool their orders?

None of these "solutions" may be practical. And of course, many of them are not really "systems questions." But they can help to unlimber your mind. You must be convinced that the system's objective is a worthwhile one . . . or an essential one. Why get a systems result that is of little value?

Once you are satisfied that the objective itself is acceptable, spell out the objective more completely—for example, as follows:

To ship goods to the customer in accordance with his instructions or in the cheapest way. To see that all shipments received on the dock by 8 a.m. are on the trucks or railroad cars and are moved out by 4 p.m. the same day. To send all "fulfilled" shipping notices for that day to the billing clerk by 8 a.m. the following morning.

3. HOW STRAIGHT IS THE CHANNEL?

The systems objective or result is your guiding star as you redesign. Steer straight for it.

The trigger point is your platform for looking at the objective. Stand up on the platform (figuratively, of course), and look *from* the point of origin *to* the termination of the activity. Then ask this key question:

How directly could we go from this trigger point (where I now stand) to the objective (that I have in focus at the other end of the systems channel)?

This visionary technique can keep you from bogging down in the labyrinth of systems details.

Note: The terms *work objective, systems objective,* and *systems activity results* all have the same meaning.

Don't dismiss this "go direct" idea lightly. Think about it. Discuss it with others. Could the system run without any paper? With no data? Without a computer? Use a conveyor belt? What work really has to be done in order to move the transaction from point A to point B . . . from the *start* to the *end* of that system cycle?

By asking questions, you and other people will begin to envision a rather direct channel, both physically and functionally, that you may decide to use as part of the new system.

The shortest distance between two points is still a straight line.

4. CONSIDER THE SUBOBJECTIVES

After you have selected the most direct route from (1) the start to (2) the finish in the systems channel, give some thought to the system's subobjectives. What records must be kept? What reports must be made?

Question: How do you identify subobjectives? How do you distinguish between a major objective and the minor or subobjectives?

Answer: Subobjectives are those that would not exist if it were not necessary to reach the main objective. *Example:* In a payroll system your objective is to pay the employee for his or her services. Subobjectives of the payroll system may be to collect money for tools the individual buys . . . to provide him with health insurance or life insurance . . . to collect money from his wages (acting for the government) as income taxes . . . to provide executives with reports on total labor expenditures by departments, reports by labor overtime, or reports on the payroll by other classifications.

Those are all subobjectives of the payroll system. But as pointed out earlier, if you did not pay an employee, all the subobjectives would disappear. Do question each one of them. You may learn that some are not really necessary. Others can be combined . . . or handled more easily. But all legitimate needs must be provided for in the new system.

When you design the new system, be sure that all systems activity is really necessary. Otherwise you will be permitting the continuation of a form of waste.

So list each subobjective. Write a brief statement about each so you can weave them into your new design.

5. THE MAIN LINE AND THE SIDETRACKS

Since a system is not visible, we can make the activity clearer if we use analogies.

The two analogies we have found most helpful in systems education include the *railroad* and the *river*. (We often speak of the system's channel.) These terms appear throughout the book. Of course, an analogy is never the same as the real thing, and we can't stretch it too far.

Let's consider the railroad analogy. A railroad has a main line track and many sidetracks. It is a total system; a transportation system. It is made up of many railroad subsystems: locomotives, bridges, tunnels, cars, tracks, stations, signals, rights of-way, repair shops, offices,

The railroad tracks provide a way for cars (like systems transactions) to move from one town to another town. Here again is a cycle—a trigger (shipping) and a result (receiving).

Every system should handle regular transactions and a percentage of *irregular* transactions. We call such transactions "exceptions" or "variations." Often they must be handled by different processing steps. *Example:* If 900 out of 1000 transactions are regular, we can "run them" quickly over the system's main line. Then we design the system accordingly.

> ☞ This main line and sidetrack idea is important. The designer must keep it in mind as he considers the systems transactions and the path they will take.

While the main line (regular) transactions go zipping along, the sidetrack transactions will move through more slowly. On the sidetrack the irregulars are out of the way of the main line traffic and don't hold it up. They move more slowly on the sidetrack because they stop at more work stations or at different work stations.

If 100 out of the 1000 transactions cannot run through rapidly over the main line, then we think of putting them off onto "sidetracks" as we design the new system.

Since the idea of a track indicates routine handling, there will be a few transactions that cannot be handled on any track, main or side.

6. THE SYSTEM CAN'T HANDLE EVERY TRANSACTION

Some transactions require *personal handling*. A capable person must give them his attention. *Example:* Customer complaints should never be handled on a routine basis. If you try this, you further irritate someone who is already angry enough to complain.

People involved in the system tend to emphasize the exceptions because these give them trouble and are hard to handle. So do recognize the exceptions.

Before you plan how to provide for the exceptions and variations, do furnish a straight line "shot" over the main line. "Sidetrack" transactions (to continue with the railroad analogy) can be taken care of later. Clear the way. Let the great bulk of the transactions move swiftly along the track. Only when that job is done should you return to give your attention to the exceptions. Ask yourself:

How should we deal with those "mavericks," balky transactions that we just can't handle routinely?

DO NOT TRY TO HANDLE EXCEPTIONS ON THE MAIN LINE! Never tangle up your main line operations with these odd balls. If you do, you slow down 90% of your transactions for no reason.

Exceptional transactions require more processing. We have actually seen people design systems that put *all* the transactions through *all* the processing steps, which may be as many as 50, whereas 95% of them could have been processed in only 8 steps.

If a high percentage of your transactions can flow through the systems channel rather swiftly, let them go. To handle exceptions you may need to design a secondary system, a supplementary (sidetrack) system, one that is slower because more processing is required.

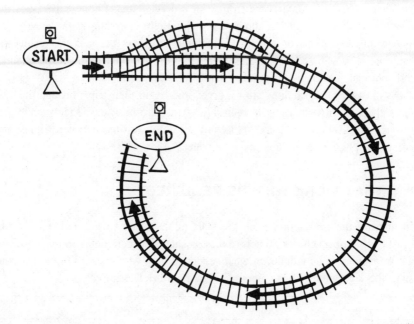

Transactions that can't go entirely on the main lines need a "sidetrack" channel. Identify such transactions.

7. LOOK AGAIN AT THE TRIGGER

Since the transactions that flow through the system have their origin at one point, look again at that point. Who "mans" that work station, that job, that post? How qualified? How well-informed?

What guards are there that prevent errors from entering the systems channel? Can all the data that people will need subsequently (later in the channel) be generated right at the start?

Is the trigger point itself right? Are you satisfied that the cycle *should* begin there? Should it be earlier, in a related but previous sequence? Or later? In other words, do you feel that the new system should cover a shorter cycle, perhaps one that has fewer processing points? Or one that has more points, in a longer channel?

Now describe the system's trigger. How does the data originate? How does the action start? Who starts it? Why? Does a related systems cycle precede this one? Data appears on what printed form? List *every* data item on that form: date, name, address, city, state, province, zip or post office codes, description, quantity, price, and so on.

Where does such data come from? An order? Letter? Phone call? Does the first operator add data from some record (a system's memory)?

Are the data items on the final document (the one that gets the result) the same items you listed on the first printed form? At what point in the channel did someone add data? Or remove data? Who uses data?

As the many transactions are triggered and begin their trips through the systems channel, how many start each day? Are there peak days? How many get through the system each day? What is the total span time between trigger and completion? One day? Three days? A week? A month?

8. WHAT WORK WILL BE REQUIRED?

In moving the transaction from the start of the cycle to the end, what work must people or machines do before the transaction is complete? In this case you list what work is *now* done, in what sequence, and who does it? In the list consider the computer as one "person." Here's a brief example:

Actor	*Action*
Mail clerk	1. Delivers all orders to order department.
Order department clerk	2. Sorts orders by product classification.

Actor	Action
	3. Checks each order for credit approval.
	a. If no credit approval, logs order on credit sheet.
	b. Sends order to credit.
	4. Sends orders to order processing.
Order processing supervisor	5. Assigns orders (by customers) to responsible order processing clerks.
Order processing clerk	6. Pulls prepunched cards for that product and that customer.
	7. Types factory order worksheet, getting punched paper tape as by-product.
	8. Feeds tape and two cards into terminal.
Computer	9. Looks up customer and product data.
	10. Writes stored information about customer on terminal's printer.
Order processing clerk	11. Types in applicable details from the computer printout on factory order worksheet.
	12. Proofreads data and initials worksheet.
	13. Etc.

You may list 40 to 50 such work steps in the working sequence.

9. CONTINUE TO LOOK FOR SHORTEST DISTANCE

Since the shortest distance between two points is a straight line, how straight can you make the new systems channel? Think about this again. Are the systems brackets perfectly clear to you now? They MUST be!

If you have described the end result carefully and you know in detail how each transaction starts, you can *ask:*

How can we provide a channel for the transaction to ensure that it goes from the start to the finish with the smallest number of work steps, the shortest distance, the lowest cost, the least time, yet the required degree of quality?

To answer that question, work your thinking backward. Start with the result. To get that result, what must people do? Critically examine each work contribution that lies between the two brackets of the system.

√ Must this work be done?
√ Could it be dropped?
√ Combined?
√ Done elsewhere?

You may have discovered that more work must be done in the new system, not less, because the present system is poorly controlled, or the frequency of errors is high. Sometimes new, better systems cost more than old, poorly performing systems. Not often, but sometimes.

What is the least amount of work people must do before reaching the result? Pick out the most *essential* job. Then the second most essential. Then the third.

Why are any other jobs necessary at all? Why is the data stored? Mailed? Filed? Transcribed? Photocopied?

Now that you've listed all work elements and know who does them and in what sequence, you can analyze the transactions as to their essential work needs.

10. ANALYZING THE TRANSACTION ITSELF

How many transactions flow through the present system each week, each day, or each month? Do they all go to each work station along the channel? Why do they have to do so? Could *some* transactions bypass a number of the work stations?

Consider work station 4. Do only 15% of the transactions have to go to station 4? What is the work contribution there? You may have found that it is only a "rubber stamp" activity. Are the approvals already taken care of? Has the proofreading already been done at a previous station? It is a characteristic of natural systems that more than one actor does the checking.

If there are 20 steps, could 85% of the transactions go through only 12 steps? Perhaps the next 12% of them can go through in 15 steps. Would only a small percentage, say 3%, really need to go through all 20 steps?

You know that a step should be a pause, a point along the systems channel where a person (or machine) does something to the transaction. He makes a "contribution of value." But sometimes people do work that doesn't really make a valuable contribution.

You'll be able to spot steps that may be candidates for elimination. You know what the transaction is. You know what the result is, and you know how the activity starts. You know the systems channel quite well. *Example:* In one complex system, we studied 100 sample transactions and found that they all went through exactly the same number of stations or work steps . . . a total of 42. But as we analyzed the transactions, we found that only 8 out of 100 had to go the long route (42 steps); 65 transactions could have been completed in only 7 steps.

The working people don't think about such things. When they "develop" a natural system, they put all the transactions in the same hopper, in the same "mental basket," and send them all through the same channel. Tough transactions, easy transactions . . . all get the same treatment.

When you're designing the new system, let the bulk of the transactions flow quickly and smoothly through the systems channel. (The main line.) Design the system so that any transactions that can't move fast are shunted out of the way and taken care of in some other manner. This is like clearing the main line track on a railroad for the high-speed, crack passenger train and shunting the slow local and creaky freight trains out of the way, permitting the fast train to roll on quickly to its destination.

Watch this: Systems also can get cluttered when people stumble over an extra tough transaction that occurs perhaps only once a year or once in two years. Then they'll run all the other 100,000 transactions through the checkpoint needed just for the special case. An analyst prevents this by instructing someone, at some point in the channel, as follows:

> If the data cluster on a transaction is not complete or does not fit the A, B, C, or D classifications for any reason, take the transaction out of the batch (out of the system). Give it to your supervisor for handling.

There are always a few transactions that defy routine handling. Arrange for someone at a work station in the channel to identify such situations. Then he can take the odd transaction out of the system and hand it over to another person who is capable of processing it.

Remind yourself what a system is. It is a plan for handling reasonably routine work in the form of transactions. It coordinates the work actions and the skilled contributions of various people. It is a way of handling work in large quantities and at low cost per transaction.

Any transaction that cannot be dealt with routinely should not be in the systems channel at all. This lack of common sense is what bogs down many bureaucratic operations. Help people to identify and switch out the tough transaction as rapidly as possible.

Note: A transaction that cannot be handled on a routine basis is a miniature *project*. Projects CANNOT be taken care of routinely by the average person who works within the regular systems channel.

Nonroutine transactions need individual attention from an experienced and capable person, such as a supervisor. There should be no problem here because the quantity of such complex transactions is bound to be small. Let a key person handle demanding cases. That's one of the reasons he is there. It is part of his job to see that the routine flow is not interrupted . . . and that the bulk of the work passes through the channel and is completed day by day.

11. DATA PROVIDING

When you know what *work* is essential to move the transaction from the start of the channel to its terminal, your next question is: Exactly what information does each person at each work station need to do his work?

Some of the data can flow through the channel, such as on a production order. Keep this data flow to a minimum. Look on the work of moving data as common information: everyone who works within the channel will need it.

But at each work station you'll find people have a need for additional information . . . uniquely needed at that specific work station. The salesman, the order clerk, the credit manager, the factory planner, the production man . . . all need the common data reflecting one transaction, such as a customer's order. But in addition the salesman needs unique data such as the customer's use for the product, other products he has purchased, or information about competitive products.

The order processing clerk needs a different set of unique data, such as a complete description of the product, the customer's preference for shipping, or packaging details. In turn, she'll pass on the last two instructions to the people who actually do the packaging and the shipping.

☞   If the new system doesn't yield exactly the needed information at the right time, the individual will have to set up his own subsystem to supply it.

"Data scrounging" is a typical characteristic of a natural system, not a planned system. How much systems memory will each person need? Won't the salesman want to keep a copy of the order he sends in? Will the order clerk need a log of "orders in"? Later won't she post each transaction "out" when she gets a copy of the invoice (indicating that the order has been shipped)?

Pick one or two pivotal work stations along the systems channel. Ask, "What are the exact and unique data needs of the person at that station?"

12. PROVIDE FOR THE THREE SYSTEMS FUNCTIONS

The data-scrounging questions bring us back to a systems principle. Your new system must provide for the three essential systems functions represented by data clusters:

1. Action data (such as the order form)
2. Memory data (such as the order log)
3. Report data

A report may be a note from the order clerk to her boss that "order 4783, due out 11-3, is 4 days overdue and is open on my log."

Reminder: A system's purpose is to get a necessary or valuable result. People, responding to the data on the action form (often an order), do their parts of the work, gradually moving the transaction through the systems channel toward the result. The "big show" of every system is to get *action*. Memory (files) and reporting are "sideshows"—essential, but still sideshows.

Memory and reporting are subsidiary uses of data. Memory (like the order clerk's log or the salesman's extra copy of the order) is a *basis* for control.

The control function, dependent on the system's memory for information, can be exercised only by a person who has the authority to redirect action when it isn't going according to plan.

The order clerk may tell her boss, the supervisor of the order department, that order 1783 appears to be overdue. She is reporting. Her memory device (the log) enabled her to spot the overdue order. The supervisor can now check with the production people to see what happened. He seeks to redirect the action . . . to correct the overdue situation. Or the salesman may follow up. Or a man in the factory may do it.

So as you design your new system, recognize that although an action data cluster gets results, you must also provide for some systems memory and some reporting. These last two functions are the insurance facets of the system . . . to ensure that the action *does take place!*

Your new system won't be complete until you provide for all three essential system functions . . . action, memory, and report.

Most systems provide primarily for action and let the system users (operators and their supervisors) rig up control logs or lists to serve as memory. Some systems analysts, particularly those working with a computer, give much of their design time to the memory (files and records), devoting inadequate attention to the quality of the action data cluster.

13. MAKE REPORTS A PART OF YOUR SYSTEMS PLAN

There are many types of reports in use . . . financial reports, special reports, routine reports. It is the last type that can and must be part of your new system . . . . an important by-product of the action.

In Chapter 2 we discussed the idea of feedback. That's what a systems report (a routine report) is—a feedback to a "controlling mechanism." However in this case the mechanism is a man or a woman, a manager or a supervisor.

The system itself is a plan. It evolves out of the combined efforts of managers and analysts. In a system for shipping, the sequence of decisions that would govern the systems action could be described as follows:

1. We will ship materials to our customers on a daily basis.
2. The action channel that results in shipment is the order processing system.

3. The shipping function consists of this work: packaging, crating, labeling, addressing, inserting packing sheets, preparing bills of lading or freight orders, calling for transportation services, loading trucks and railroad cars, and notifying the billing clerk that the shipment has been dispatched.
4. The daily average of shipments will be 52 a day: 260 per week.
5. Based on past output measurements, the work will require a staff of one supervisor and six other persons to handle the work load. This is 280 man-hours a week.
6. To help adjust to fluctuating work loads (from a daily low of 33 shipments to a high of 74), the shipping section is permitted a span of up to two working days from the time of receiving an article from finished goods stores until the shipment is in transit.

Those are the *plans* for the shipment activity . . . the expected results. The measurements are based on past results using the present system (the methods now in use, the present floor and shipping dock layout, and the required paperwork).

The shipping supervisor and his boss, the traffic manager, are the people who need feedback on the actual results. The supervisor and his six subordinates know, at the end of the work shift, exactly how many shipments they have made. If a peak of 90 orders come into the section on Thursday, the staff may be able to get only 55 or 60 of these on their way that day. Then the supervisor should ask his boss: "Can we get some temporary help?"

The traffic manager, who is not out on the shipping dock, must react to data . . . to information. He will need to know the results less often than does the supervisor. Possibly a report once a week is enough. If so, however, your new system must provide for such a report.

Where will you tap the data for this report? Could the data be generated in the computer? Or should the source be the billing operation? (It is usually best to have reports on the performance of one functional unit come from data generated in another functional unit.) There's less chance of a whitewash report.

What will such a system report include? There are just six essential elements.

1. SUBJECT. What does the report cover? Tell *exactly:* "customer shipments."
2. ISSUE DATE. If the report covers the previous week (July 10th through the 14th), the issue date should be on July 17th, the following Monday.
3. PERIOD COVERED. Be exact. Say "from July 10th through the 14th." If

the report says, "July 10th to the 14th," it is not clear whether the 14th is included.

4. PLANNED RESULTS. The plan was to ship 260 orders.
5. ACTUAL RESULTS. How many orders were actually shipped? It may have been 238.
6. DIFFERENCE. The difference between plan (260) and actual (238) is 22. Is this difference within a reasonable tolerance?

The traffic manager can decide. He may want another, a different report . . . one that tells how many orders have been in the shipping department for over two working days.

The analyst has a great opportunity to render his user-managers a vital service . . . systematic reporting on results. Recognize this:

☞   It seldom happens that a manager will fail to do something about a "bad" situation . . . if he is informed!

If any manager is informed, yet fails to make corrections consistently, he soon loses his managerial rank.

So design your new system with good feedback as a part of that system. Good feedback consists of information on actual results, with a comparison to planned results . . . a report that reaches a person who has the authority to redirect the action or to change the plan.

Do not send a systems report to any man or woman who could not redirect action if such redirection is called for.

The redirection can be informal. The traffic manager, looking at his weekly report on shipments, could pick up the phone and say to the shipping supervisor, "Good morning, Bert. I see the total orders shipped were down a little last week. Did you clean up all that you had on hand?"

If the shipping dock *was* cleared, that may be the end of it. But suppose Bert says, "Boss, I'm sorry to tell you this, but there were 38 orders that we'd had over two days that were still here on Friday. We couldn't get them all out." Now some redirection of action is likely to ensue.

When a manager has that type of knowledge about the results from people in a section under his jurisdiction, he knows where his attention is needed.

Happily, good systems reporting tends to get a self-correcting effect. Do you think Bert wants his boss on his neck? Of course he doesn't. So he is likely to do what he can to avoid missing the plan. He knows that if he and his people do not hit the plan for the week, his boss will be talking to him on the following Monday. Even the six people in shipping are likely to want to avoid putting Bert on the spot.

If an unexpected large load of orders arrived late Thursday, Bert would know right then that he and his people couldn't ship them all by Friday afternoon. He might call his superior at once and say, "Bill, we just got a big load we didn't expect. And to get all the orders out by Friday night, we need some help. How about that little lady from your office who wrote up the bills of ladings for us five weeks ago? Could you spare her to help us on Friday?"

Good systems reporting is a beautiful aid for good management.

If your organization's workload is expanding, good systems reporting informs management when additional employees are needed. This could also work in reverse and tell management that the workload has fallen off and that the department now has too many employees.

Often reports are an afterthought. They are not made a part of the systems plan. But things *will go wrong* in any system, and redirection will be needed. The effective analyst recognizes this, and by the way he weaves in the memory and reporting facets, he provides for quick redirection of the action.

14. YOUR CREATIVITY PEAK

When a systems analyst develops, after much effort, the "just right" idea for a new system, other people often see it as a relatively simple answer to the problem. They may say, *"Why didn't we think of that?"*

People in the organization who do not do systems work are not aware of the process that the effective systems analyst goes through to get an easy-looking answer. One analyst, who had created a number of highly profitable systems for his organization, was asked why he was so effective. He replied:

I'm willing to sweat first . . . and I know that the inspiration will come.

Systems analysis can be hard work. Every analyst, somewhere along the classic path, feels some discouragement. He has his black moments when he wonders if he'll ever get the answer to this tangled problem.

But the professional analyst knows that if he keeps at it, the answer *will* come. He must continue to pour factual inputs into his mind. He continues to do pick and shovel work—searching through files or having repeated talks with the operating people.

He will spend lonely hours analyzing and puzzling over the data he has secured. He'll chart and rechart the data. He will sort and resort the information. Finally the answer will come!

The answer may come like a bolt of lightning. The analyst may be plugging away, and suddenly the way to go is perfectly clear. That is his creativity peak. When they arrive, good ideas will tumble out in profusion. So he keeps plugging, knowing that the moment of revelation will come.

15. BRING ALL THE IDEAS IN FOCUS

Can you now visualize the new system? Are some of the ideas still out of focus? Fuzzy? How do you now bring everything into sharp focus?

Draw another grid chart that reflects your vision of the new system. First show the trigger and the result. (At the extreme left and the extreme right.) Now you have the brackets of the new channel. They may be the same as those in the present system.

At first show only the main line that runs between the trigger and the result. You can show how the exceptions (sidetracks) will be handled later, on another chart.

Fill in with work statements reflecting the essential processing steps between the two brackets. Word these statements carefully, briefly but adequately . . . and in sequence, of course. Who performs the work at each step?

Will the computer serve? Treat the units of the computer as individual "actors." Write up, in main line sequence, exactly what each work unit will do. For example:

Key in the data
Edit for accuracy
Sort into processing sequence
Move into central processing unit
Process. Spell out what: compare, add, subtract, divide, multiply, and update
   the record.
Store. Put record away on disk
Print. As hard copy? Another action form?

Turn to your new action form. Lay it out. Check the title. Is it meaningful? Have you decided what will serve as the key or pivot data item? A name? A Number? A date? A case?

Will the new memory cluster (record) be different? Whether it will be kept on the computer's disk or on a posted card, is it designed for ease of *reading?* That is what a record is for. People are supposed to be able to read it and then *use* the information. So it must be highly readable.

Only as you get these elements into tangible form can you communicate the detailed plan to your associates, to the people who took part in your study and suggested better ways.

You are constructing your systems plan from intangibles like programs transactions, triggers, systems channels . . . and from policies, functions, flows, work authorities, controls, or responsibilities—all mental things.

The plan immediately becomes more tangible when you chart it. Make as many elements of the system visible as you can.

Give your associates graphic evidence of how the new system will work. Consider using flow charts, bar charts, even pictures. Use some straight explanatory copy . . . but not too much.

Once you convert your plan to black and white, the new system is no longer an unborn brainchild. Your plan is then something real . . . something that can continue to live.

16. DEVELOP A TITLE FOR THE SYSTEM

Every project needs a name, a "handle" that everyone can use. Put some zip into the title. Of course it must be accurate, but it doesn't have to be dull. Don't label your new plan "Project 382." That's a dull title. To get people to accept a new way of doing things, the plan's title needs some emotional excitement built into it.

Make up a "selling title." What are some BENEFITS that will accrue to the people? Or to the bosses? Or to the organization? For your title, use words that reflect the strongest all-around benefit.

Systems analysts have used titles such as these . . . *Streamlined Production System . . . One-Writing System . . . The Clearing House Plan . . . Short-Cut System . . . A Customer Service System . . . A Three-Day Turn-Around System* (this is good if the old turn around was 10 days).

When you make up a grid flow chart reflecting the new system, don't make it too detailed. Don't show where every last copy goes into a file. Show the main line flow first. You can indicate the variations in a subsidiary chart.

You've worked on the key action form and the new record. Will there be other new forms? New reports? Show samples of them, at least in pencil form, ready for typesetting. Include in your tangible display of the intangible new system any and all related documents . . . new procedures, new policies, new computer program (show the detailed logic chart, not the detailed coding steps).

17. COORDINATION IS NEXT

Wrap up all the details. Write. Chart. Demonstrate. Describe. Get the complete plan in the most tangible form possible. Wrap up all the details into one package. Now the "dream," the visualization of the new system, is in tangible form. Next, check it out. You are now at signpost 9.

Reminder: Don't avoid pin pricks. (These may hurt a little.) Take your plan, as complete as you can get it, to your associates in the project. Let them do you the favor of shooting holes in it—if they can. Don't take it to a friend who will tell you how good it is.

Get various individuals to concentrate their criticism on *their portion* of the work. They are work experts only on their own work. You're the expert on "hanging it all together." Listen to a person's comments on other work phases, but you'll get the most value if you get each person to stay with what he knows. He should tell you whether the new plan will help him do *his* job.

Make a note of every comment you get. What you're really asking people is:

Will this new way work better than the present system is working for YOU? Will it eliminate any of your present problems?

Go right through the systems channel doing this. Go from one work station to the next . . . in sequence. You'll be amazed at what you will learn. You'll

Before you finalize the design, check it out with the people who are in the system. They are the work experts. Listen to them.

probably want to revise some segments of the plan.

You, and the involved people, are immersed in the system. You need some more objectivity. So take the plan, and all its physical evidence, to someone who is NOT involved in that system. Ask him: "Will it work?"

Don't be thin-skinned about it if he shoots down any element of your plan. He is doing you a favor. He can prevent you from making errors you don't want to make. Listen to all the reasons why some parts of your plan won't work.

After you are through with this pin-prick exercise, you may revise elements of the plan. You may agree with your critics in some particulars. In other things you may decide to stay with your original plan.

This pin-prick test for your plan is just the first of a number of checks or tests that you'll make before the system is in and operating.

This is more than the coordination phase of your work. It is also one more opportunity for you to keep the operating people involved in the project. Most of them will appreciate your meticulous care with details. They're taking the role of consultants . . . of work experts, which they are. People like this. Too often no one listens to them.

18. EXPERT OPINIONS

Did other people serve as advisors while you developed the system? Auditors, programmers, methods men, industrial engineers, machine company or forms company representatives, floor layout architects, . . . perhaps an outside consultant?

Does the new system seem ready to run . . . from the viewpoints of those specialists?

19. WRAP IT UP

Now bring all details together. Clean up every facet of the new system. Consider all the suggestions. Decide what to accept. If you don't accept an idea, contact the person who gave it to you. Explain why. The man or woman will appreciate your courtesy.

If you are not going to do all the work personally, decide how you'll delegate the detailed jobs. Who will do the programming? Test the program? Furnish the typical transactional (real-life action data) data clusters to make sure the jobs will run.

Who will write the procedures? Design the forms? Finalize the master grid chart that reflects the new systems channel?

If you'll need new machines or equipment, who'll contact the vendor (through Purchasing, of course), prepare the specifications, and get a tentative promise on delivery date?

When you have cleaned up all elements of the system, you are ready to move down the classic path to the next step — the presentation of the new plan to members of management. That will put you at signpost 10.

Your new forms can be in pencil. Do not print them yet. Chart the new computer program, but do not code it. Do "roughs" on most of the other documents.

Here are some facets of the new plan to have in semifinished form:

☐ 1. The new master grid chart and new subsystem charts.
☐ 2. Sketches of all new forms.
☐ 3. Roughed-out copy of any suggested new policy statements.
☐ 4. Written summaries of the two systems, the present and proposed one.
☐ 5. Highlights of the differences between the present and the proposed system.
☐ 6. New machine requirements, costs, and delivery dates.
☐ 7. Benefits the new system will bring, contrasted with lack of such benefits now.
☐ 8. How the new system ends the problem that kicked off your study originally.
☐ 9. How it will eliminate or minimize other problems you've uncovered.
☐ 10. What retraining will be necessary for the operating people.
☐ 11. How much the changeover will cost.
☐ 12. How soon it all can be done (installation date).
☐ 13. What do the people in the present system think of the new plan?
☐ 14. What undesirable factors will be eliminated (errors, lack of control, poor service, waste, high cost, low morale, etc.)?
☐ 15. Drafts of any new procedures.

Get these all in shape before you move to the next signpost on your classic route: *Presentation.*

PRESENTING THE NEW SYSTEM

Your new system is finally in mental focus. You (and the people who helped you) know what changes you should make in the present system.

You can now explain the new system. To do so you have charts, forms, descriptions, programs, reports . . . all tangible reflections of the system, which itself is not tangible.

Before you install that system you have another signpost on your classic path—number 10: presentation.

1. FOUR INTERESTED GROUPS OF PEOPLE

The detailed knowledge about your design cannot remain in your head. You must explain the configuration (exact shape) of the new system to at least four distinct groups of people:

1. Your own "team"—the men and women who helped you develop the system. Most of these people are users of the present system.

2. Any persons who were not included on the team but who will be affected indirectly by the system . . . those in related systems.
3. The manager or managers who can give you an OK to install the new system. This approval will include any required finances.
4. People who served as advisors . . . an auditor, a consultant, an accountant,
   a methods man, an industrial engineer, operations research people, a data
   processing manager, a computer programmer, even representatives of systems machine or other vendors.

Much of this final checking with others can be quite informal. This is not the
case for the third group, however . . . the approving executives. Focus on that
group. Prepare your new plan for them, and then you'll also be able to explain
it clearly to people in the other three categories.

2. WHAT DO THE OPERATING
PEOPLE THINK?

One of the first concerns of a manager is the opinion of his operating people.
Do those who must operate the new system accept it? A manager knows (or
senses) the importance of this acceptance.

The acceptance factor is less applicable to the portions of the system that
enter the computer room. The computer will accept, within the limits of its
design, anything that you instruct it to accept. But there are people in computer
rooms, too.

What is the reaction of the computer systems analyst? The programmer? The
manager of computer operations? Do they see the new system as an improvement over the old?

Concentrate your attention, however, on the people WHO WILL RUN THE
NEW SYSTEM. Who "pulls the transaction trigger" in this system? What is
his reaction? How much does he know about the new plan? Consider the key
people who are located at subsequent work stations. Do they feel confidence in
the new design? What is the attitude of their bosses? And their bosses' bosses?

If you've handled your survey properly, your operating people are already
reasonably well sold on the new system because you went out of your way to
be sure it was *their* system, not just yours! You let them *contribute* ideas, and
you made *use* of most of their contributions. You acknowledged and credited
them for their suggestions.

You have now arrived at the stage where you must sell those executives who are the approving authorities, the higher-up executives. It may be that only one man is in the position to say YES or NO.

3. MAKE ALL ELEMENTS VISIBLE

We know that a system is an invisible form of work activity and that no one can actually see a system. Executives do not often buy an idea that they consider vague.

So how do you make the invisible visible? How do you give the new system enough "visibility"? You can convey your vision of the new system by providing:

1. A written summary of the new plan
2. A summary on the problems in the present system
3. New form records and reports
4. New procedures
5. A brief description of new machines or equipment
6. Printouts of new computer programs
7. Charts that depict major "before and after" factors
8. Any key job outlines
9. Your installation schedule, in broad form
10. The benefits the organization will enjoy when the new system is operating

You may add other tangible elements. *Example:* If the executive likes statistical tables, you can present some of these.

4. DON'T TELL ALL

When you studied the present system, you gathered a great deal of information. Do you expect an executive to read it all? Be assured that he will not. Even if you put all your information in good order, it has no place in your proposal.

A proposal is NOT a dump for all the information you gathered during the survey.

There's only one place for all the data you picked up during the survey. That is in your working files.

Your presentation summary is an *abstract* of what you propose to do about

Don't tell all. The busy executive doesn't want to know every detail.

the present system. To do its job, it must be a highly selective document.

When the key man gets your proposal, what are some of the things he'll definitely want to know?

1. Specifically, what WAS the problem? (He may not remember.)
2. The extent of your survey
3. The solution you propose
4. The benefits he can expect for the organization
5. The benefits his department or his operators will get

The man new to systems analysis may want to impress a key executive by showing how much work he did in the study. So into the man's office he trundles an armload of notes, written information, charts, form samples, and all the other data and samples he picked up.

No good. No executive has hours to spend sifting through data. As you develop your proposal, use this general guide:

Tell as little as you can, yet make the key idea of the new system clear. Tell briefly why the new system will be better than the old.

5. GIVE YOUR NEW SYSTEM
A LIVELY TITLE

Let us stress the matter of titles again. What are some of the most striking changes you are going to recommend? Or what are some of the most attractive results? Pick a word or two from such ideas. Can you work them into your title?

Words that can make your title effective are words that will express worthwhile *benefits*. That's the question that most executives ask: "What good results will we get?" Think a moment about that word *benefit*. It means something that the organization, the executives, the people, or the customers, get *from* your new system.

Benefits are not the methods of your new system . . . they're the *results!* Typical benefits could include lower costs, faster service, more control, reduction of man-hours, more economical buying, reduced inventory, larger profits, higher morale of the employees, released working capital, lower taxes, more flexibility, reduced risk, more income, and more profitable income.

Those are general suggestions. Make your benefit ideas apply to your system as specifically as possible. If the benefit is "reduced inventory," how much will it be reduced? Give this information in dollars or percentages . . . $17,850 or 10%.

The purpose of the title is to grab your man's attention immediately. Some people think a title that identifies the project is enough. Not so. Identity is fine, but the title is also a selling device. A dull title such as "Project Number 76 on Auditing for Property Control on the Accuracy of the Records," identifies the system, but that's all it does.

Your selection of the title words will depend on what your executives know about the problems in the present system. For example, if they know that the present system requires a span of 10 working days for a transaction to· go through to completion, you could use a title such as this:

New 7-Day System for Processing Orders

The contrast between the 10-day period that the managers know is now required and the 7 days that you promise will get their attention because they are anxious to give the customers faster service. Hold your title length to between three and six words.

But be sure that the executives *do* know that it now takes 10 days to process an order. If you are in doubt, remind them.

6. EXECUTIVE APPROVAL

Do other executives approve your new system before you install it? Is there a committee in the executive ranks (such as the corporate operating committee) that approves such major changes? Does your own superior give his approval? Will a special budget approval be required?

In some cases the three or four department heads whose people run the system will give the "executive approval."

However if you are a manager rather than an analyst and the system is one that will operate entirely within your department, you are the final authority. As long as your subordinates are satisfied (be sure they are—consult with them) and will accept the new system, you are ready to plan the installation.

Many systems flow through several departments, and often other people, in other departments, are involved. The new system may require a large expenditure of money. This will call for high-level approval and a revised budget. It is well to keep all top executives informed on major system changes.

If they are given a chance to see the plan for your new system before you install it, executives will better understand that there may be minor hitches and bugs in the system. They will understand that these can be readily corrected.

Otherwise, these management people may hear about weaknesses that show up early in the new system. They may be inclined to abandon the new system before it has had a chance to operate and prove what it can do.

While operating people may ask questions that are quite detailed, executives will have a different viewpoint. They make up a different audience. Your presentation to them should reflect a consideration of this difference.

7. EXECUTIVE INTERESTS ARE DIFFERENT

Executives are aware that they are stewards of one section of the organization . . . often a department. They are also stewards of large segments of valuable resources, especially time and money. They have an obligation to the owners to be sure that these resources are well used or invested.

Executives are not enthusiastic about making changes that are just changes. Most top people are apt to ask direct, down-to-earth questions (How do you KNOW this system will save $37,000 a year by reducing errors?).

Men and women at the top are sensitive to such items as reduced inventory, more income, good customer service, reductions in labor problems, better control, more profit, improved employee productivity, good employee wages, and lower costs in other items.

Note: About presentation to executives: they are not likely to want a lot of detail; they probably will be bored by it. They may even dismiss you before you have had a chance to give the entire story.

We say *usually* they don't want details. A few executives do. This is particularly true if the new system operates in an activity with which one executive is quite familiar. In the past he may have been a worker in that area.

Some men or women may ask for detailed backup. *Example:* You quote a cost savings figure. They'll want to know how you arrived at that figure. Be sure what you're offering as a new system is sound . . . and that it will work. If one benefit seems too good to be true, you may be asked, *"How* will the new system accomplish such a good thing?"

If you tell all, the busy executive will be inclined to push your proposal aside.

Be prepared to answer in detail when presenting the new system's plan to executives. But do not offer detail. Have it available, that's all. If your worksheets are in good order, in numbered and titled file folders, you can dig up any detail within a few minutes. Or another person can be prepared to do it for you.

Do not go into the same detail you provided the employees. If an executive wants a detailed answer, he will ask for it. DON'T OFFER IT.

Even the timing of an executive presentation is different. You may need an hour or longer to explain the system to the people who will run it—the operating men and women. It is likely that you have only 15 to 20 minutes to present the system to a group of top executives.

Observation: Many men and women fall down badly presenting a new systems plan to executives. This failure (or partial failure) seems to be due to three factors.

1. DETAIL. The person presenting the ideas doesn't understand that executives are not interested in the same specific details that operating people must know.
2. NONSIGNIFICANT ITEMS. The speaker is unable to extract information that is significant (to executives) from the mass of information he used to plan the new system. So he throws the entire system at the listeners and bores them.
3. JARGON. He is not careful to use plain English. Rather he uses technical terms or even technical initials (ANI, MIS, CPU, CRT, DOS, PERT, I/O, COM, OS).

Remember: Even if the operating people accept the new system, it cannot come to life until key executives also accept it.

8. WRITTEN OR SPOKEN?

There are two ways to make a presentation: (1) with written information and (2) by talking to people about the new system.

Use both ways. Don't depend on just one. On my first big systems job I made the mistake of putting a big sheaf of papers (200–300 pages) on an executive's desk, hoping that he would read them. They remained in the same position on his desk for two weeks. The cleaning man wiped the surface around it. The executive never read it. I learned then that people working in an executive capacity will not read such tomes.

A "tell everything" written presentation will yield no action, no approval, no go-ahead. And all your work up to this point will be wasted.

That is why you should also personally explain this new system to both groups (operators and executives) on a face-to-face basis. You should also make available summarized written information to be examined later.

Presentation is a subpath along your classic route to systems improvement.

Consider the "subpath" that your face-to-face presentation is to take. Time it for 15 minutes. Practice. Give the presentation two or three times to other people. Or do it in front of a mirror.

Don't try to race through, spewing out a lot of information. Pick out the four or five key points that will interest top managers. Present these carefully. Speak slowly. Show your confidence in the new system.

9. BENEFITS AND LOSSES: WORDS THAT MOVE MEN

Words, of course, represent ideas. And two special ideas can move people to take a recommended action. One is a *benefit* word. The other is a loss idea expressed by a *loss* word. Both have the power to "move men." Let's define them:

A BENEFIT is something that a person or persons will gain by taking a specific type of action.

A LOSS is something that a person or persons will suffer from until steps are taken to avoid it.

Let's explain. In the selling process the customer must *buy* and then *use* the item offered to get the benefits. Benefits are desirable and valuable. People will not receive these benefits if they do not take the recommended action.

Thus two ideas make people want to "buy" a new system. One idea is positive and the other is negative. The problem you encountered in the present system was causing some losses . . . some undesirable results (negative).

People will often "buy" the new system to eliminate the negative situation—if they are convinced that the new system will stop the loss. Thus the elimination of a loss is a "sales mover."

On the positive side, is the new benefit a tangible goal, such as "save money" or "serve better." Words that express benefit ideas are also powerful sales movers.

Here are 30 benefit ideas that systems analysts have used to sell their new systems:

1. More productive people
2. Realistic, useful planning
3. Higher productivity of employees
4. Lower costs
5. Meet people's current needs
6. More economical buying
7. Lower, but adequate, inventory
8. More innovations
9. Increased service to the community
10. More profits to the owners
11. Employee morale increased
12. Reduce need for working capital
13. Significant reports on operational results
14. Better use of capital
15. Lower taxes
16. Reducing the operating expenses
17. Lifting debt restrictions
18. Fast payout on equipment
19. Paperwork reduced
20. Fewer man-hours per output unit
21. Effective project control
22. Flexibility
23. Increased growth
24. Safeguard proprietary information
25. Reduced risk
26. Will reduce cost from ____ to ____ (be specific)
27. Work areas are safer
28. Answers to difficult problems
29. Good credit
30. Lower credit losses

Do any of those benefit ideas fit your situation? Or suggest benefits that your new system can provide?

Now let's look at some negative words that suggest losses.

1. Inventory too high
2. Inventory stock outs
3. Unfavorable ratio of inventory dollars to sales dollars
4. Serious errors
5. Increased costs of error corrections
6. Low output from obsolete machines
7. High cost of maintenance
8. Higher taxes
9. Low employee morale
10. Poor planning
11. Mismanagement
12. High interest rate
13. Crowded conditions
14. Low use factor on expensive equipment
15. Lost time
16. Lost customers
17. Losses of money
18. Waste
19. Constant emergencies
20. Floods of complaints
21. Partially obsolete inventory
22. Failure to take discounts
23. Labor unrest

10. THE PHYSICAL FORM OF THE PROPOSAL

How will you reach your approving executives? Entirely by using a written proposal? At a meeting? We suggest that it be a combination of a written proposal and a visual presentation in a meeting!

Include a written proposal. One page is enough. Write in summary form, giving the answers to these questions:

1. What was wrong in the present system
2. Why that situation caused the problem (losses)
3. How your new system will correct the things that you found wrong in the present system
4. The benefits we should expect to get
5. Present losses that will be avoided

Consider supplementing your written summary with some of these devices:

1. Physical evidence. Could you use a fabricated part, an assembly or a letter from a customer?
2. A photo (enlarge it).
3. A chart of a new floor layout.
4. A bar chart that contrasts ideas such as:
    a. old way—147 data items
    b. new way—52 data items
5. A revised organization chart, showing the old way in RED and the new way in BLACK ink.
6. A proposed new policy.
7. A draft of your new key procedure.

11. PRESENTATION AT A MEETING

To get fast action, ask your boss if he can convene the key executives in a meeting. Ask for 20 minutes of their time. Present your new systems plan in 15 minutes and answer questions in the time remaining.

Then consider how you'll use the 15 minutes to make it count. Get an easel that holds a pad of white paper approximately 2 feet wide by 3 feet long. You'll use this paper for flip charts. The sheets will also serve as your speaking notes.

First use smaller sheets (8 ½ × 11 inches) to rough out what you'll put on each large sheet. Remember you're doing a *poster* job here. Consider the brevity of the billboard. Use only a few key words on each sheet. Do NOT put on the big sheets everything that appears in your typewritten proposal.

Put the title of your new system on the first sheet. This starts the benefit idea. Flip the top sheet over the easel to reveal the second sheet. Here you write out the problem . . . in a few words. Use big bold black letters, at least two inches high. Step back from the easel. Can you read those words easily from 20 feet back? If not, make the letters larger until you can see them 20 feet away.

Logically your third sheet will tell the cause of the problem in eight or ten words. On the fourth sheet tell briefly how you made the study. Stress that you went to the work experts, to the operating people. On sheets 5, 6, 7 tell how the changes in the new system will overcome the problems that exist now. This may take three to five sheets. Use one sheet to list the present losses.

On one of the sheets, toward the end, stress the benefits of the new plan and *why* it will provide them. Expect one of the managers to challenge you here . . . maybe in detail. If you have one of your project team members with you,

Use large, poster-size sheets to present the new system. They tell the story and also serve as your speaking notes.

he can have your organized detailed folders with him. Then he can give a specific answer.

Make it a good 15-minute show. Interesting. Fast moving. Dramatic. Supplement the flip charts on the easel with projected transparencies on an overhead projector or with individual charts that you hand out.

Should you send out your written summary beforehand? This is a good idea—in theory. But I've found that most executives do not read the material before the meeting. So summarize it. Then, after your easel presentation, give them the prepared copy.

If you think it will be more helpful, you can use an overhead projector instead of the easel. Prepare 10 or 12 transparencies. You can also have half as many backup (detail) transparencies. Show these only if you are asked a detailed question.

One of the sheets or transparencies can show the new action form (typically filled in). You can also use such a "form facsimile" in explaining the new system to the employees involved. You can show the new grid flow chart on a transparency.

Can you get some help from an artist or a draftsman? With a bar chart you could show the losses incurred because of the old system, then contrast those losses with the benefits that will be obtained by using the new system.

12. TYPICAL TIMING

Prepare your presentation carefully. Decide exactly what information is essential. What seems to you to be the most logical sequence for your presentation?

How much time? We recommend 20 minutes . . . 15 minutes for presentation and 5 minutes for questions. Here is a typical time schedule for such a presentation:

Sequence of Easel Page Numbers	Subjects	Minutes
1	The problem and the unhappy results (losses)	2.5
2	Your study, working with the involved people	1.0
3	Brief description of present system	2.0
4	Highlight the changes in new system	2.0
5	Benefits to expect from it	2.5
6	How soon they can get it (schedule)	1.0

Sequence of Easel Page Numbers	Subjects	Minutes
7	The cost	1.0
8	Repeat the loss and then the two strongest benefits	2.5
9	Ask for the approval	0.5
	time for presentation	15.0
	allowance for questions	5.0
	total time	20.0

13. DON'T BE WISHY—WASHY

Some analysts who are new to systems work offer executives a number of different routes. This is a mistake. Such analysts are telling executives, "We're not sure what we ought to recommend. So would you please complete our staff work by selecting the way that we should go?"

Do not offer any such choice. YOU select the one best way. You must make that decision. By now who knows more about the system than you do? Certainly not the executives. Also you've had a lot of solid advice (if you have been working with your team members). You've also listened to advisors.

Yes, there are always alternate routes. If you have other approaches in mind, or somebody suggests them, keep them in written form but tucked away—with your background materials. If you have considered these ways to go and decided against them, make notes on *why* you decided against them. Put those notes in a folder titled REJECTED ALTERNATIVES.

If someone later suggests that you should consider one of the other ways, you can say, "Well, we did consider that but decided not to go in that direction for the following reasons. . . ."

14. ASK FOR THE ORDER

In any form of selling, when you think your customer is convinced that he should buy your product, you ask for his order.

When you make your proposal to several executives, you do it for a purpose—to get their approvals to install the new system. So the executives do think your idea is a good one. Where do they sign? Have you provided a place for one or more approval signatures?

In one company a form titled AUTHORITY FOR EXPENDITURE is a master approval form. The systems analyst always brought it along with his proposal (and it was all filled out, of course).

If a top executive approves the new system by signing that form, all the minor approval actions follow in the wake of this single master OK.

Do not ask a top executive to approve every item * in your plan. He is not concerned with the details. He just wants the resulting benefits. Let other people approve requisitions, OK forms, approve job outlines or procedures.

15. WHAT TO DO WITH A REJECTION

Sometimes your idea for a new system *is* turned down. You may feel that all your work up to this point has been wasted. Not necessarily. Most likely the turndown will be for reasons you couldn't control. If this is the case, you should *know* those reasons.

Often when a new system plan is pigeonholed or actually turned down, the rejection may be temporary. Action on the plan may be postponed or deferred. The timing of your proposal, unknown to you, may have been wrong. If your plan is stalled or rejected, find out *why*. Then if you did make a mistake, you can avoid making the same error in the future.

As you think about the rejection, here are some questions you can ask yourself and discuss with your team members:

1. Did we bring out the strongest *benefits?*
2. Was our timing faulty? Did we try to present the new system when other matters or *emergencies* were pressing hard on the executive?
3. Was the *budget* too tight?
4. Were our *machine* requirements too expensive?
5. Was some influential user *opposed* to it?
6. Did we try to make *too big* a change? Should we try again, selling smaller chunks, one at a time?
7. Was our proposed change too *radical?* Untested?
8. Did some people oppose the change because it affected their *empires?*

---

* If your plan is rejected, you might want to try again, selling one step at a time, if this is feasible.

Even in failure, you can gain a measure of success. The idea is to benefit from any rejection by holding a sort of post mortem. Often a plan rejected today will be eagerly sought after in a few months.

But the chances are that you'll get the approval immediately or shortly thereafter. Often an executive puts off an immediate answer to give himself a chance to confer with a member of his own staff. If the executive wants further time to "consider," ask him for a decision date. Say, "May we have your answer by next Wednesday so we can get the long-term requirements under way and we can start gaining the benefits as soon as possible?"

If the man feels that he needs more information, offer to supply it. When you do get the go ahead, your next step is to plan the *installation* of the new system. That is signpost 11. You are nearly at the end of the classic route to an improved system.

CHAPTER 11

INSTALLING THE NEW SYSTEM

You are now far down the road toward a new system, having just passed the "presentation" signpost. You've presented your plan for the new system, and the people in authority have said to go ahead.

1. YOU INSTALL IT

At the installation stage some systems planners (whether analysts, consultants, or industrial engineers) feel that they can turn the job of installing the new system over to the operating people and their supervisors. If they do, the probability of the new system failing is high. The line supervisors and the operating people are busy getting out their day's work. Furthermore, not one of them is fully aware of all the in's and out's of the new plan. They do not understand all facets of the pattern. They concentrated primarily on their own work requirements during the survey. Without guidance from someone who knows all facets of the new system, they cannot install it and get it working.

☞   That is too much to expect. YOU install it.

The operating people can run the new system, but they can neither plan it nor install it. They are experts at routine work but know little about the techniques of project work And installing a new system IS a project!

That's why you, as the analyst, must recognize that (1) installation is a project task, and (2) project handling techniques are different from routine work techniques.

2.   PROJECT WORK IS DIFFERENT

We said that project work is different, so let's take a few moments to see why it is different. Ever heard of 100% overruns in money and 200% overruns in time on big projects? Sometimes such results are disastrous. They happen because the people trying to run the project are not knowledgeable as *project managers.*

So let's take a quick look at project work. People in organizations carry on two distinct types of work, routine and project. When the new system is operating the people will be doing routine work. Probably 90% of all work done is routine. That is the way our organizations get just about all day-to-day work done . . . through routine handling of most transactions that flow through.

But a project is different. You cannot "run it" the way you do routine work. There are no well-worn paths, no measured work units, no cycles of action . . . and no identifiable systems channel to follow.

Your entire survey job, so far, has been a project type of work. Developing a new system is a *project* type of work, whereas running an existing system is a *routine* type of work.

The number of failures in project work is large. Such projects often involve millions of dollars in losses because people did not know what a project is. As a result, they tried to run a project by managing it as though it were routine work.

The step of systems installation is a pure project. It requires one man to run it (presumably you), serving as the project manager. Be clear on this:

Success depends on how the project manager runs the project. If he fails as a *project manager,* the project itself will fail, too.

Projects, under the wrong person, can overrun by double the planned cost or the planned time. Such failures are common when the project manager is not competent to control the job, when he doesn't recognize that a project is not routine work, or when he has done a poor job planning and estimating.

The essence of the result-getting project management lies in two activities:

1. Intensive, detailed planning
2. Close, constant, and disciplined control

You develop a plan you will use to control the many individual jobs, breaking the big job (systems installation, in this case) down into a number of smaller jobs.

3. DANGERS IN PROJECT HANDLING

Installing the new system could be risky business (as could any project). Why? Because a project is a type of work that does not readily forgive mistakes. Let us emphasize again (it is so important) the difference between systems *routine* work and systems *project* work.

1. In routine work there are a series of transactions going through a known systems channel. Since the channel is cyclical, someone can catch a mistake and correct it on the next batch of transactions. Thus routine work tends to be "forgiving."
2. In project work (such as installing a system) there is no forgiveness. There is no next trip through the cycle. You do the job one time only and you're finished. The errors had better be minor, minimal in number, and quickly corrected. You get no second chance. The success or failure depends on "one turn of the wheel." At the end of the turn you'll have either triumph or disaster.

Most of us who have worked in organizations for any length of time have seen systems that flopped. Later people laughed at them. Actually, systems failure is a tragic thing. Perhaps the systems plan itself was good, but the man who directed the installation didn't appreciate what he was up against. Or, he may have had a sloppy attitude toward his job, failing to recognize the need for great care, alertness, drive, and the tremendous amount of detailed planning that must go into a successful installation.

4. NEW IN: OLD OUT. WHEN?

Now that your new system is going to replace the present one, just how will this come about? Will you drop the old system out of the picture on, say, Monday morning at 8 a.m.? Is that really feasible? Perhaps the new system involves from 100 to 150 different changes? After you've planned them, how can you implement them between Friday afternoon at quitting time and Monday morning before starting time?

Recognize that the business of the management system must go on. Transactions must continue to flow through the channel. Installation sounds easy, but it isn't . . . even if you know how.

Don't forget Murphy's law: Anything that *could* go wrong with some element of the new system as you install it, *may* go wrong. The solution is to anticipate, and be ready to prevent or to quickly correct such a breakdown.

5. BREAK DOWN THE INSTALLATION JOB

Installation is the big job, THE project. To plan and control all aspects of the big job, identify all the subjobs that make up the big job.

One subjob may take one person one hour to do. Another job may require 100 man-hours. Here is an installation check list that systems analysts have found helpful. All these 58 possible jobs probably won't apply to your project. Some others that are not listed here may apply to you. A checklist helps avoid overlooking a job or two.

1. New computer program (for the application itself)
2. New software (for the required operating systems)
3. Coordinating changed details with the people affected
4. Designing new action forms
5. New records
6. New reports
7. Changed policies
8. New organization charts
9. Announcements sent to employees involved
10. Publicity on the system for the entire organization (this allays people's fears)
11. New machines
12. New equipment

13. New supplies
14. New physical layouts (may require moving, carpentry, electrical, plumbing, painting, etc.)
15. Changes in work station duties
16. New lighting and/or power
17. Changed acoustics
18. New terminals
19. Telephones changed
20. Flow charts for training
21. Preparing other material for training
22. Testing everything new
23. Providing for moving
24. Retraining sessions
25. Getting temporary help
26. Getting approval for overtime
27. Approval of any necessary capital expenditures
28. Scheduling money needs in the operating budget
29. New file cabinets
30. Outside guidance or help from vendors or from consultants
31. Piloting (testing one part of the new system)
32. A suggestion system employees can use to propose quick changes on installation day and in the following week
33. Provisions for quick error detection and correction
34. Job outlines for new or changed pivotal tasks
35. Employee transfers
36. Setting up detailed time schedules for each job
37. Work assignments to individuals
38. Coordination of installation activities (hold meetings)
39. Bids on supplies or equipment
40. Coordination with union representatives
41. Temporary supplies
42. Disposal of unused systems documents (forms, records, etc.) relating to old system
43. Hiring people with newly required skills
44. Coordination with branch offices at remote locations
45. Communication with customers, if they are affected
46. Communication with vendors, if they are affected
47. Communication with government agencies that affect you
48. Decisions on individual cutover schedules

49. Early audits of the new practices
50. Setting up information booths or designating phones to use during installation (have someone "man" a message center?)
51. Providing supervisors with new work output standards
52. Doing work method studies at key work stations
53. Creating a list of priorities
54. Developing helpful decision tables for the computer, people, operators, or supervisors
55. Instructions for computer or terminal operators
56. New procedures reflecting the "main line" of the new systems channel
57. New procedures that reflect "sidetracks" or variations
58. Estimating time and money needed to complete each subjob

In a large systems installation, the detailed jobs may run into the thousands. It can be a major project effort just to keep them all under control. Some projects are so complex that the manager should call on the computer to keep him informed daily.

Observation: A checklist such as this will start your own thinking about the individual jobs.

In some cases, even the job listed should be broken down further. *Examples:* Under checklist item 11, NEW MACHINES, your new system may require six such machines. Each one might become a separate job. Under item 1, NEW COMPUTER PROGRAMS, you may require four of these . . . and these might become four separate jobs. Likewise under item 47, COMMUNICATIONS WITH GOVERNMENT AGENCIES, the job may require different types of communication with the city government, the regional planning board, or the state, the county, or federal government. Item 31, PILOTING, could be a subproject of its own.

Question: Can a system analyst without experience in project management successfully install a complex system?

Answer: If it is complex, probably not.

Advice: If you haven't planned and run a major project before, get someone who has run a project successfully to serve as your guide. Perhaps one of your team members. If you can't get guidance from within, ask for funds to get an outside project consultant. First plunge in and do all the planning you can on your own. Then get your guide's reaction before proceeding further. Develop a list of subjobs, and have him check the list (rather than having him develop the list).

6. TIME AND MONEY

The two factors you must control are time and money. Time is more important than money, so let's consider it first.

Time will defeat you on your project unless you control it. (Actually, you cannot control time, which moves along at a steady pace despite anything we humans can do. You can only control what can be accomplished within the framework of time.)

Pin down the time required to do each subjob. For instance, how long will it take to do the training job? Who will plan the training and how much time will he need? *Ask him.* Who will write the text matter or other written training aids? How long will he need? Who will prepare the slides or transparencies? How long will each of the subjobs take?

Consider equipment. What new equipment will you need? How long will it take to get delivery after you order it?

If you are changing programs on the computer, how long will it take to reprogram? How long will it take to test the new programs, using typical transaction data as information inputs?

You may not know the answers to many time questions, but other people will. Consult them.

Are you planning to change the physical layout in the office? This could be quite a subproject in itself. Such a layout change will be made up of many subjobs. Each takes some time. *Example:* How long will it take to get materials after you order them?

Someone must spend time on certain layout subjobs. Someone must draw the floor plan, showing doors, electrical outlets, lighting fixtures, and ventilation outlets. Someone else must break down these drawings into bills of materials (lists of the materials required). A buyer will order these materials, probably doing some shopping to get the best price at the acceptable quality level. It will take time to get all materials. Some items may be hard to get and may take more time than you think at first. Although you can order necessary lumber and hardware one day and get these materials two or three days later, some items may take two or three weeks. Make sure.

Ever heard of inventory stock-outs? Items misshipped? Strikes? Shortages? Disasters? Of course you can't plan for *all* bad luck, but you should plan for some.

If you don't know the answers to hundreds of questions such as these, YOU CANNOT RUN THE PROJECT SUCCESSFULLY. Let that statement sink in. Why? Because it is made by the voice of experience: our personal experience. We might even say our bitter personal experience.

The right way to run the project is to first plan thoroughly how much time and money each subjob will take.

Start by listing every subjob you can think of yourself. Next, sit down with other qualified people and show them your list of subjobs. They will undoubtedly add to the list. They may suggest some of the subjobs you have listed are too large and need further breaking down.

7. TYPES OF TIME

Since other people handle most of the installation subjobs, be sure there is a common understanding of the meaning of "time."

From a project viewpoint there are different kinds of time. Consider

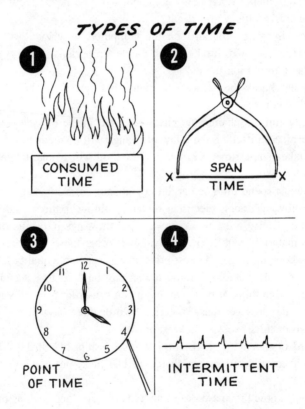

The project team members must communicate with one another, particularly when speaking of time.

1. Consumed time
2. Span time
3. Point of time
4. Intermittent time

If the forms designer uses 15 man-hours to design the new SALES ORDER, that is *consumed* time. If it will take the printer 20 days from the time he gets the order to deliver these forms, that interval is *span* time. When the forms designer takes five minutes to read the proof copy and approve it, that is a *point of time*. It is less than six minutes (one-tenth of one hour). The man-hour is the measuring unit, and the tenth is the smallest unit.

If a job requires constant monitoring (such as checking on the progress of one critical job several times a day), that is *intermittent* time.

Span time is the vital kind of time. Even if no one in your organization is consuming man-hours, you must wait until the vendor or supplier does his job and the ordered articles arrive.

8. WHO ESTIMATES THE TIME AND MONEY NEEDED?

When you have the time estimates on all the subjobs, you may find time spans that vary from one day to 100 days. It may be that the 100-day job is the one that will be the span that governs the installation project's deadline.

Who should give you an estimate on the time and the money required to complete each job? Ask the person who is going to do that job. He should know, if he has done similar jobs in the past. Since he is also the person who will execute the job, if he does the estimating he will be committed to that time and that amount of money. If you impose your estimates and later find that both time and money were underestimated, he can shrug the error off as your responsibility.

Estimating money is not difficult. Of course the estimator must *know* the exact cost. No guessing. If you follow these rules, money troubles should be minimal.

It is the misuse of time that gives the most trouble in a project. If time is not handled right, the monetary costs will also rise rapidly. And time is the equivalent of money. *Example:* For job 27, the estimate is 40 hours for time and $100 for materials. If the 40 hours will cost $15 per hour, the total time cost plan will be $600 (40 hours × 15 dollars) plus $100 dollars for materials. The total is $700. If the total *actual* time proves to be 55 hours, the total cost shoots up to $925.

If the total cost will be $925 instead of $700, it is a 32% overrun. What will your project look like if you have such overruns on all the subjobs?

Look for dependent links on each subjob. Ask, "What other job must be completed before we can start THIS job? In turn, what other jobs are dependent on the completion of this job?"

Confer with the people who know. Go to the work experts, those who have done the subjob before. See if they agree with the way you have sequenced the jobs. When you are reasonably certain that you have done the best you can, give each job a short title and number it. Arrange the jobs in the sequence in which you or the other people will *start* to do them.

9. PUT THE SUBJOBS IN SEQUENCE

You have listed all the subjobs that someone must do before you can install the new system. Look over those subjobs.

What job must be done first? Can you start the 100-day job at once? If you find it will take 15 man-days of work on other jobs before you can even start the 100-day job, you know you're up against a time span of at least 115 days before you can install the new system. Since you'll need a safety factor, add 12 days (10%), giving a total project span time of 127 days.

Continue to think that way about each of the subjobs. Where does each job fit in the sequence?

Some subjobs can be done at any time within your master schedule. These are "floating jobs." Most jobs will link to other jobs in a chain of dependencies, however. *Example:* You can't perform job 33—TRAINING before you finish job 32—TRAINING PLANS AND PREPARATION.

Most subjobs thus are linked to other subjobs. You may find that job 16 can't be started until you have completed job 10. But jobs 12, 13, and 14 can be run in parallel—go on simultaneously—if you have 4 people with the necessary skills to do the work.

10. DEVELOP INDIVIDUAL SPECIFICATION SHEETS

For each subjob make up an individual specification sheet. Do this for any job that will take one hour or longer. Sounds like a lot of detail? It certainly is. But

PROJECT JOB SPECS.
FORM 1032-C

JOB NO.   JOB NAME

    27-14   Ordering Forms: Combined Purchase Order & Rec. Report

ELEMENTS OF JOB   TOOLS NEEDED

    1. Designing combined set
    2. Writing, printing & bindery spec
    3. Marking copy
    4. Writing purchase requisition

MAN DAYS (CONSUMED)   SPAN DAYS   ASSIGNED TO

    0.5 (4 hours)   97   J. Ray Moore

DEPENDENCIES

PRECEDING JOBS	SUBSEQUENT JOBS
24-10 Studying data needs	28-4 Test on terminal printer
25-3 Coordinating with Wilson,	29-1 Training operators in use
Burns, Alvera and Manson	

SCHEDULE DATES

CAN START BY   September 18

MUST START BY September 23

CONTRIBUTORS	QUANTITIES	COSTS	QUALITY
J.T. Wilson	50,000	$51 per M	Last copy
Pedro Alvera			clear
J.E. Duffy			
Ellen Burns			Exact
			machine
			spacing

OTHER REQUIREMENTS

    Printer's proof   Bindery specs developed
    Test carbon dummy   Packing: 5,000 sets to box
    Check spacing in machine

Consider using job spec sheets for each subjob in the installation project. They'll help you control the details.

don't try to slide over it. Remember, *one* sheet for *each* job. The sheet will contain the following:

1. The job number. This will be a start-sequence number. The job that starts first is number 1, the job that starts second is 2.
2. The name of the job. *Example:* "Order new input cards."
3. Elements of that job. Here you expand the title and tell exactly what the job includes.
4. How many man-hours (if that is your unit of measure) will it *consume?*
5. The *span* days, if they are different.
6. Who will do the job?

7. What work must be done before you can start this job?
8. The start of what other jobs are dependent on the completion of this one?
9. Actual (calendar) start and finish dates. These will go on your Gantt * chart
10. Costs.
11. Materials or other requirements.
12. Quality standards.
13. Will the job need testing?
14. Who will perform the test?

11. GANTT CHART: PICTURE OF THE PROJECT

To plan and then to control your installation project, you need a constant view of the project as it moves along. Since a project (like a system) is not normally visible, to manage it you must make it visible. Use a Gantt chart * for this purpose. (Some people maintain that the Gantt chart is old-fashioned, insisting that you should use PERT or CPM charts † to run a project. Those useful modern charts can be generated and updated by a computer.)

* This type of chart was developed about 1915 by Henry Gantt, associate of Frederick W. Taylor, father of scientific management.
† PERT = program evaluation and reporting technique, CPM = critical path method.

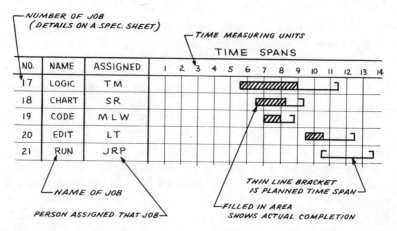

The Gantt chart's details permit you to plan the installation, then follow the progress as you execute the plan.

Yet the Gantt chart still has its place. It is the chart you use to plot each subjob against a time scale, usually a calendar. Be sure to distinguish between the Gantt chart and the grid chart: they look somewhat alike, but their purposes are different.

There are many versions of the Gantt chart. Some are offered as magnetic boards, boards with strings, bars, slides, or colored signals.

The elements of the Gantt type chart include:

1. Two columns at left: one for the job number and one for the job title
2. A third column for the name of the person responsible for doing this job
3. A time scale in the selected unit of time measurement (hours, days, weeks, etc.)
4. A "where we are" plumb bob, labeled TODAY

List the subjobs down the left side of the chart, in sequence, according to their *start* times. Who will handle the job? Put his name in the next column, opposite the job.

When will the job start and when will it be finished (calendar dates)? Show your start and finish planning with a thin line and two brackets.

GANTT CHART

JOB NO.	JOB NAME	DUTY OF	TIME IN DAYS

A Gantt chart is your device for coping with the calendar.

Everything you show on the Gantt chart is in terms of *span* time. If you order a machine that requires 30 days for delivery, you show this 30-day span on the chart. On the other hand, if plotting and coding two new computer programs will consume 10 man-days, but you will assign this task to two programmers, the span time will only be 5 days. That's what you show on the Gantt chart.

As the job progresses, you show this progress by "blocking in" a dark bar, which represents the actual accomplishment on that job.

Do NOT show manpower requirements on your Gantt chart. Use a separate chart for that purpose. Use your Gantt chart only to show span times as it relates to the calendar.

To coordinate all the work that must be done, and then to keep his installation project under control, the project manager can use three distinct types of charts:

1. A time chart, one that relates each job to the calendar (Gantt)
2. A job relationship chart (PERT or CPM)
3. A manpower loading chart

The value of a chart is that it provides you with vision. You can't possibly manipulate all the job specification sheets and get a view of your entire project. But through charts you *can* do this. The chart enables you and your team members to see activities they could not see in the ordinary sense. We will not attempt to explain the subsidiary charts here (PERT or CPM or manpower loading).

12. BE PEOPLE CONSCIOUS

Knowledge of project control techniques is essential for the project manager handling a systems installation. But don't get hung up on techniques alone. Be conscious of the people who are involved in the system.

People fear change that they don't understand. We all fear the unknown. If you have been keeping people informed as you developed the new system (with many of them working with you as part-time team members), the possibility of such fears will have been erased at the installation stage.

People will not fear changes in the new system if they understand each change and the reason for it. Many have contributed their ideas about what should be changed. Therefore they not only accept the new system, they want it.

At installation time you can see how important it is to do your systems work—not just on an "engineering and design basis," but primarily on a *participation* basis!

The right kinds of workers (and they are numerous in our organizations) dislike clumsy or wasteful operations. If they see a better way of doing a job, they will be for it. People resist change only when they don't understand it, or when it affects them adversely or hurts personally.

The two essential ingredients of a really great system are:

1. A well-conceived plan that will reach the system's objective with the least amount of effort, distance, cost, and with the fewest possible errors.
2. The eager acceptance of the people who are to operate the system.

Those two ingredients are equally important. If your new system does not have the backing of the people, no matter how well planned, trouble lies ahead. On the other hand, if the planning is poor, if you didn't design a system that goes as straight as possible to the objective, even the acceptance of the people won't improve the design.

Often when we are ready to install a new system we give much of our attention to charts, schedules, new computers, new disk files, new terminals, software, programs, forms, procedures, and all the rest. But those are just inert ingredients. There is no life in the system until the people themselves are "installed in it" . . . which is one way of putting the idea of people acceptance. If the people who run the system are "well installed," your new system will live, breath, and get results for your organization.

13. SHOW CONCERN FOR THE PEOPLE

Often a new system requires less manpower than the old one. Or it calls for skills different from those used in the old system. Will the man who is now involved in the system feel enthusiasm for the new plan? Or will he secretly (or even openly) work for its failure? The basis of reasonable people acceptance of the new system is your organization's real concern for the welfare of the employee who is now doing a job within the old system.

This concern can't come just from you. It must come from the person's supervisor and from top management as well.

Assuming that your organization is concerned about the welfare of its employees, how do you *demonstrate* this feeling? Just talking about it won't do the job. However this concern will show if these suggestions are followed.

1. Keep each employee informed on what is happening.
2. If he must shift his skills or secure new skills, tell him how he can help himself.
3. When there will be no change in his work in the new system, let the employee know.

4. If it doesn't already have one, urge your organization to issue and apply a policy that says, in effect: "No one will be laid off, lose status, or experience a reduced salary because of any systems improvement changes." To be useful it must be a policy that top executives back. (If management doesn't mean it, don't bother to state it.)

5. Suggest that during the survey, supervisors keep their regular work forces slim by getting temporary help to keep the work going, if some experienced people have left the organization.

6. Urge the personnel people and the direct supervisor to use attrition to help reduce the work force (if you know it's going to have to be reduced).

7. There will be a peak period of work when you change over from the old system to the new. For this need, get and train part-time employees or those secured from outside employment services.

14. SKILLS AND TRAINING

Skills fall into the following categories: (1) the skills you'll need to install the system and (2) the skills required in the new system that were not required in the old system.

Give some thought now to training people to operate the new system. Know what training is necessary. What skills will be changed, added, or subtracted from the present skills of people running the current system?

How will you provide this training? Individually? In classrooms? Demonstrations?

Pivot your training around tangible items such as the documents or the forms . . . or the programs, the procedures, the action forms, the records, the input forms. If the new system involves the use of terminals, the format in which information will be put into the terminal can be presented during a training session. Can you bring a terminal right into the training room?

Use visual aids. You can use slides on a screen, or a large blowup placed on an easel in the training room. Reinforce any such visual presentations by providing each person with 8½ x 11 inch copies of the blowups or slides. Pass these out at the meeting, or put a kit of aids in the hands of each individual as he comes in.

Allow some time for questions. If you don't get any from the people, ask *them* questions. See if they can answer questions on some of the new techniques you have just been telling them about. Before you know it, you will have lots of questions and discussions.

How do you transfer working knowledge from one mind to another? Set up a training program that pivots around tangibles such as forms or procedures.

Listen patiently to any beefs, to any feelings that are negative. Do not argue. If people have a feeling that there will be trouble, or that something isn't too good about the system, listen. Listen attentively. Listen respectfully. Don't snap back any answers such as, "Oh, we've already thought about that. We threw that idea out long ago because it isn't valid."

Such an answer will arouse resentment on the part of the individual offering the suggestion. At the least, it will dry up his comments. He thought the idea was new. And to him it was. Much better to say, "That's an interesting suggestion." Then go on to explain what would happen if you followed it. In any training, talk about the new system in terms of the people's jobs and their problems, and their functioning in the organization. If others will do the training, brief them on the approach you'd like them to take.

One of the most effective ways to explain something new is to start with something old. Go from the familiar to the unfamiliar. The people know the present system. In what way does the new one differ from it? Point out the differences.

As you face up to the problem of retraining people, you'll recognize the value of not making any change in skills unless the new system really requires it. It's much better to use present skills, slightly altered, than it is to make many major changes that are of doubtful value.

15.   WALK THE CYCLE BEAT

This is the day! This is the morning! This is the hour! Your new system is
ready to be born . . . finally installed. So get your feet off your desk. Get
down there on the working floor. Watch that new system being born . . . and
stay there all day, perhaps most of the week.

When a new system is going in, the people will be both stimulated and confused. Be there to answer their questions. Now is the time to make everything
go right. If you aren't there and people start doing things wrong, the situation
will be hard to change later.

You are thoroughly familiar with the length and breadth of the systems channel . . . you know the side flows and the outflows . . . you know the links to
other systems channels. You know about the exceptions.

So personally walk from the start of the systems channel (trigger) to its end
(result). How are the transactions doing at work station 4? Are they moving
along as planned at station 8? Are any bottlenecks developing?

If the systems channel threads through the computer, are the inputs accurate?
If you are processing by batches, are these batches moving into the processing
stages as you planned? If you have installed a real-time system (the records and
the data reflecting the actions are identical, within seconds of each other), is
the data from the action stream being recorded and processed, thus changing
the records "instantly"?

You will encounter some pessimists who are convinced that the new system
will never work. They wonder how soon you are going to give up on this new
systems nonsense. Listen to them. Try to cheer them up. Don't expect everything to be music and flowers. Expect to encounter growls and kicks; some
people will even say, "We should go back to the old system."

Smile. Be silent. Don't argue. Look sympathetic and look thoughtful but
maintain your own courage. Either you and the people who worked with you
designed a good system or you didn't. Don't falter at this point. Recognize
your strength. You have the authority of knowledge. You knew that old system
backward and forward . . . and you know the new one better than anyone else
in the organization.

16.   THAT LEARNING CURVE

Do you know that when you first install the new system, productivity (output
per man-hour) WILL GO D O W N? Expect that to happen. The people must

slow down when they start to do unfamiliar jobs. Even though they may be trained, they will not develop skill and speed until later.

Is it essential that the normal productivity rate be maintained? If it is, have a crew of temporary people ready to move in and keep things going. Your knowledge of the learning curve principle tells you that while productivity goes down at first, it will gradually increase and eventually outstrip the productivity of the old system.

CHAPTER 12

THE COMPUTER'S CONTRIBUTION

1. FOUR MARKS OF A MANAGEMENT SYSTEM

Do you believe that what you have studied is really a system? Is your redesign a true *management* type system? Here are four earmarks of a management system.

Mark No. 1   It has an identifiable trigger . . . the work station where the systems action starts.

Mark No. 2   Each transaction that flows through the system's channel is

160

	represented by data . . . a cluster of data, usually on an action form.
Mark No. 3	There is a traceable systems channel.
Mark No. 4	At the end of the channel there is a valuable result.

That result, at the end of one management system's channel, may serve as the trigger for a subsequent management system.

2. HONEYMOON WITH THE COMPUTER

The computer must be the most talked-about machine ever developed. Some people love it, some hate it; many people think it is too hard to understand, so they delegate its use to the technicians who do know how it works.

From the viewpoint of our modern management systems, we owe a great debt to the computer. It took the computer to open the eyes of management (some managerial eyes are only half-open, even now) to see what the management system is all about.

By getting down to the nitty gritty of how data can be handled on a machine, the systems thinkers (among our many practitioners) began to admire the fact that people (clerks) handled data so well in the past. A clerk did not have to be told when to lift the pencil and where to position it on the paper before writing. But the machine does need such detailed instructions. So in effect we have always had many fine computers called "clerks."

How did a clerk process an order? Before we could have the computer do this job, we had to analyze the minute steps . . . steps so tiny that the clerk didn't recognize that he (or she) was following such steps.

Managers have always thought of clerks as representing "overhead." They were considered "nonproductive." So when the computer salesman arrived with his "people-eliminating machine," management listened . . . and bought.

To whom did managers entrust the running of these new electromechanical monsters? At first to the technicians, to "the people who understood them." The result was a financial fiasco. For a decade hardly one computer installation in a thousand paid off.

As people eliminators, the first computers were a complete flop. They required not fewer people, but more . . . and better paid. Today computer costs are mainly for personnel, usually in the 60 to 90% range of total costs.

The early computers were run by technical people who usually didn't know the business of the organization. All their attention went to the machines.

Data processing is "labor intensive." The computer brought us one clear message:

> Look! This is a world run by information . . . by systems. With the right information, in the right form, at the right time, man can really *manage* his resources and his business affairs.

So such taken-for-granted clerical actions as "processing" came under the scrutiny of a new breed of men and women—systems analysts. These people, unlike the head-in-the-machine technician, saw the system and the computer as a new, marvelous information service available to the entire organization—not only to the accounting department, but to managers in all departments and at all "levels."

Thus through the computer and our early mistakes in its use, we learned about systems . . . especially about a unique but commonplace type—management systems.

3. THE CONTRIBUTION PRINCIPLE

Do you want to design a *great* system or a series of great systems? Then observe this systems principle: Each resource used in the system must contribute to the final result of the system's activity.

No deadheads permitted. This principle applies to the computer. It applies to the operating people, to any other machine, and to any piece of equipment. NO RESOURCES WASTED! No "Let's do as the Joneses do" foolishness. No "putting it on the computer" because you've got a computer and your central processor has spare capacity.

Take a hard look at every element of the system. Make no blind assumptions that anybody or anything is necessary to carry on the transactions in the system. Each element must contribute.

Your thinking in relation to things and to machines should be very hard-boiled. If one of these factors is not contributing enough, scratch it. However when it comes to people, take it easy. You naturally have a concern for each individual's welfare.

If a man is not contributing what he could or should at one work station, it may not be his fault. The situation may exist because management has not made a systems study for a long time, and waste has crept in or duplication has occurred at this work station. So you do everything you can to ease the burden on people who must be shifted around or retrained so that they can make a worthwhile contribution. They may be transferred, retrained, or their contribution may be revised so that it becomes significant.

4. OTHER WONDERFUL WORK
THE COMPUTER DOES

Anyone who has visited the North American Air Defense Command (NORAD) comes away in awe of the information power of the 20 large computers that, second by second, "process" information about what is in orbit around our globe. These machines sort the significant facts from the many insignificant facts concerning the 3500 satellites now circling the earth. It is interesting to know that an astronaut's glove and his flashlight are also out there whirling around. But that fact isn't significant in terms of Canadian and American defense.

Deep under the solid granite, bombproof Cheyenne Mountain, the American and Canadian officers watch our skies every minute of every day. They couldn't do this job if it weren't for their information-providing "servants" . . . the electronic computers and the network of communications that feed information into them.

There are other, more commonplace uses for these electronic machines. *Example:* Large earth-moving machines are high-cost-per-hour items. They must be kept at work. If they break down on a construction site, the cost rises very rapidly. To prevent most breakdowns, contractors, loggers, and large farmers use a computer-supported parts program that works like this: Samples of oil and grease from the machine are sent to a parts supplier's laboratory, where the samples are analyzed for microscopic parts of metal in the oil or grease. From this analysis the laboratory technician uses a computer to predict (within a high degree of accuracy) when each wearing part will fail.

The user of the equipment reacts to this report by ordering the parts before they are needed. Then parts are replaced before the predicted failure time or by having them on hand at the construction site. Thus the replacement parts are available, and in a matter of minutes the machines can be back on the job.

On a large poultry farm in California, the most nutritious, yet least expensive diet for egg production is determined by a computer, which directs the blending of the corn, millet, soy beans, vitamins, minerals, and so on. The computer changes formulas as costs change or as the hens grow and the weather changes.

What is our present world like? With the computer age, we have spacecraft such as Pioneer 11 visiting the Sun, Jupiter, Saturn, Uranus, and Neptune. Its magnetic readings, mass and density recordings of these far-off planets in the universe, are beamed back to earth. Then a computer converts these electronic pulses into meaningful information, even into pictures.

Process computers are still a different breed. The processing requires a continuous flow . . . such as the manufacture of gasoline from crude oil, the grinding and separating of corn, the distribution of natural gas, or an automatic phase of manufacturing.

Other wonderful things the computer can do (besides management types of work) include:

1. Playing chess
2. Playing or composing music
3. Giving a voice response
4. Playing tic-tac-toe
5. Forecasting income
6. Working a problem that has many variables that can be changed
7. Providing an answer to a mathematical problem
8. Simulating real-life conditions such as landing an airplane
9. Retrieving scientific data by subject and cross-indexing
10. Working engineering problems

11. Working chemical problems
12. Producing pictures or artwork
13. Guiding a missile
14. Serving as an educational machine for an individual student
15. Answering a person's inquiry (printout or display)
16. Tracking missiles, satellites, or aircraft in the sky
17. Answering questions on astronomy
18. Analyzing information against previous data, as in a medical diagnosis

What do all these computer jobs have in common? Information. They all use and provide information. The world of computer usage is so vast that we must say sternly:

Our interest in the computer must, in systems analysis work, be limited to the question, "What can the machine contribute to the *management* system?"

5. DIVIDE THE WORK AGAIN

Even the work that the computer can do within our management kind of system should be further divided into

1. Superclerk work
2. Management aid work

Let's look first at the computer's value in doing clerical work on a superclerk basis. When the volume of transactions is high . . . when the work is routine, dull, and repetitive . . . people shouldn't have to do it. It is office mule work. The best working mule we have is the computer. It has these characteristics:

It loves a big workload (much of the time, even in time-sharing, the processor is waiting for work to do) . . . it works fast . . . it is accurate . . . the machine is never bored . . . it doesn't tire or feel any late afternoon fatigue . . . it never complains . . . it rarely has time off for illness or vacation (just a short shutdown for maintenance, a few hours a week).

Here are some of the earmarks of superclerk work that may make it a logical computer application:

1. Large VOLUME of transactions, 55 or more each day, 15,000 or more each year. The heavier the transactional volume, the more likely the job should be on the computer.

2. SAMENESS in the handling of the transactions. The processing consists of going through the same series of work steps for each transaction.
3. ARITHMETIC. Quantities can be added, subtracted, divided, or multiplied.
4. STABILITY. The routine process isn't likely to change often. Once your system is programmed for a computer application, you have a financial investment that you can use and use and use.
5. HIGH ACCURACY. The computer makes relatively few errors on its own. Most "computer errors" are human errors.
6. TIME. If quick response is necessary for the success of a system, the computer is often the only way to accomplish it. *Example:* Airlines reservation systems.
7. TRANSCRIPTIONS. The computer excels when information must be copied into various formats within a single system or between related systems. For example, an employee's pay change would affect the personnel history system, the payroll system, and the tax accrual, payment, and reporting systems.
8. STATIC VERSUS VARIABLE INFORMATION. When a large amount of the information flowing through a system is static or constant (seldom changes), the computer is a useful tool. In a payroll application, for example, the employee name, number, hourly or monthly pay rate, job classification, address, and deductions . . . are all static types of information. For hourly employees, hours worked in the pay period may be an example of variable information.
9. INFORMATION AS A REUSABLE RESOURCE. Once information from a system exists in a machine-readable form, its existence affects the feasibility of using the computer-provided data in the design of other, related systems. For example, if the accounts payable system of a company is using the computer, this influences the feasibility of using the computer in the general accounting system. A large percentage of the information handled in a general accounting system is generated through various aspects of the accounts payable function.

Conversely, if your system requires little arithmetic, is not routine, or involves a low volume of transactions, and if you feel that there are no error-making problems and if the processing sequence changes frequently . . . then the computer, used as a superclerk, probably *cannot* contribute enough value to your system to offset its cost.

As a *management aid* most computer installations are running about 20 years behind their promoters' promises. Great were the office automation promises made in the 1950–1960 period. The computer was to be a manager's first assistant. It was a giant brain, a decision maker, a magical black box . . . it was the greatest problem solver of all time. One widespread statement: "Get a computer and you'll run rings around your competitors."

There were many *other promises*. *Examples:* The computer can predict your future, tell you what's happening in the organization now, warn you of trends up or down, provide reports on anything by any category. Fast. Accurate. Easy. Cheap. People headaches eliminated by eliminating people. Middle management would soon be useless, since the computer can take the place of supervisors and foremen.

All noisy dreams. Actually most computer installations in the first computer decade (from about 1953 to 1963) lost money. They didn't decrease people needs, they increased them. Even as a clerk replacement, they cost more than they saved. And at first the computer failed almost utterly as a management aid.

People seemed to sense that the computer *could* make a contribution that would eventually outweigh its cost—if they kept on trying and if they invested more in fancier or more recently developed equipment. They did, and the decision finally paid off. Most computer installations in use *today* do pay. Some still do not.

Observation: There are still millions of systems in use today that cannot *profitably* use the services of a computer! Be careful. Most computer installations today do pay because some analyst first did a "feasibility study" to measure the costs versus the benefits.

Seldom can a computer installation pay its way if you put only one system on it, such as the one you've been working on. On any computer you will normally find at least eight system applications such as the following:

Payroll	Invoicing
Accounts receivable	Inventory
Accounts payable	Sales analysis
Purchasing	General ledger

Any one of these management systems could be run by office clerks using files, typewriters, pencils, charts, tables, and adding machines or desk calculators. What is clerical work? These words describe clerical activity:

write, copy, proofread, do arithmetic, read, sort, separate, gather, file data (put away), retrieve data, summarize, compare, edit, make copies, list, report.

People can do that type of work. So can the computer. It can and does serve well as a superclerk. As a management tool, the computer is just beginning to fulfill some of the promises made in 1960.

6. WHAT MANAGEMENT SYSTEMS ARE MOST USED?

What management systems do people most often run on computers? Across Canada and the United States, the most used management systems, in decreasing order of quantities used are as follows:

Payroll
Sales analysis
General accounting
Inventory
Budgets
Order processing
Credits and collections
Personnel records
Production control
Sales forecasting

Our purpose here is to focus on one subject: the management system. What can a computer do for a management system? To concentrate on our type of system, let's ignore for the moment all the other wonderful types of work that the computer can do.

A computer is *not a system,* even if many people think or say that it is. The system also gets mixed up (in some people's minds) with subjects such as methods, procedures, policies, practices, individual job instructions, job outlines, functions, and organization practices.

7. CONCENTRATE ON INPUTS AND OUTPUTS

Now let's turn our attention to the physical side of the systems activity that pivots around the computer. The technological developments are so numerous,

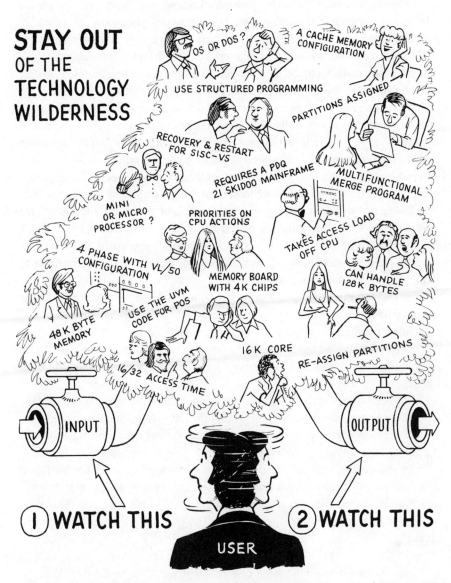

Avoid the technological complex. Give your attention to the computer inputs and outputs.

and they come so fast, that even the people engaged full time in coping with these changes and improvements can hardly keep up with them. And the person who is not a specialist in dealing with data processing equipment, software, or programming can hardly be expected to keep up with these developments.

So the user of the system, the man or woman who puts information into it and gets information out of it, shouldn't attempt to reach a thorough understanding of the technical details of data processing on a computer.

But if you are not already aware of the basics of electronic data processing, it will be helpful to consider the two most important functions from the user's viewpoint . . . the inputs and outputs. Information that goes into the computer is of concern to you. So is the information that you get out.

Your main problem is to communicate with a technical expert. These people communicate quite well with each other but not so well with nonexperts. But be patient, and don't let them give you information you don't understand. Be honest: "I'm sorry, but I do not understand what you're telling me." Don't feel ashamed of this. If it was the other way around, you could throw a lot of shop talk and mysterious initials at the computer professional concerning your work, and *he* wouldn't understand.

Two garbled messages aren't going to do anybody any good. You want to get top performance out of the system, particularly out of the automated part of it handled by the computer. For this, communication is absolutely essential. Recognize that the technical expert is usually a dedicated person. He really wants to help you. But he often doesn't know how. Try to communicate with him.

Computer professionals study teleprocessing, virtual storage, job control languages, operating systems, multiprogramming, structured programming, split screens, optical character recognition, computer output microfilm (COM), and the use of new software developments.

Even the development of the correct "lease or buy" contract for hardware and software is a major and a specialized job. It is not a do-it-yourself situation. Call on the people who know the many aspects of the computer. This way you don't have to know the operating details. You can ask the computer specialist:

What can the computer do for the system that we have developed? What, specifically, can it CONTRIBUTE? What, specifically, will it COST us to get that contribution?

Tell the computer professional what information you want the system to provide. Ask him if he can arrange his computer complex to supply it.

Avoid the vast wilderness of computer technology. Concentrate your major attention on the two activities of *input* and *output:*

1. What data will people put INTO the computer segment of the system?
2. What information can they get OUT via the computer printer or the tube display?
3. What is the COST to put this information into the system and to process it?
4. What are the BENEFITS that the organization will get from using the computer?

Answers to the last two questions should be specific and to the point. It is true that many things *can* be done on a computer, but your comment could be, "So what?" It's like the glove and the flashlight of the astronaut. It's interesting to know they are circling around out there, but of what practical benefit is the knowledge?

8. THE COMPUTER IS FOR THE USER'S USE

There is the story about the man who would always "tell all." The advice was: "Don't ask him what time it is. If you do, he'll tell you how to build a watch."

This "tell all" fallacy often applies to education on data processing. When a user wants to know more about a computer (so that he can make better use of it), the technical man tends to tell him far too much about the computer, providing information well beyond what the user needs to know. Probably a million users have been through a course in programming and not one has ever had an occasion to write a program.

The systems user should be interested only in *what* the machine can do. Naturally the technical man is intentionally concerned with *how* to do it. Here are some examples of the type of "inside information" that a user doesn't have to know:

how to compartmentalize the central processing unit's high-speed memory to permit several jobs to be processed at once . . . how to change digital impulses to voice grade impulses to go over a telephone wire—through modems . . . how to sort records (magnetic data clusters) . . . how to merge records . . . how to write a program . . . how to read a program . . . how to select software . . . how to debug a program . . . how to use software . . . how the processor works . . . machine languages in binary . . . programming languages (COBOL, RPG-II, FORTRAN, BASIC) . . . virtual storage (high-speed memory arranged to provide more memory than the machine really has) . . . data bases . . . processing and calculation speeds . . . cycle times . . . memory sizes . . . bits and bytes.

A car owner (user) can drive his automobile without understanding the mechanical aspects of the vehicle. What he wants is to *use* the automobile to transport him from here to there.

The user must assume the same attitude toward the computer. Learn enough about what it can do, then stop. Let the technical man handle the technical problems. There are plenty of skilled specialists to deal with the technical aspects of the computer, and the user doesn't need to be a technical expert, too.

Perhaps it is fascinating to know that a properly programmed computer can beat the average chess player within 30 to 50 moves. Interesting. But useful to a management system? No!

Thousands of technical people are busy figuring out how to manage complex networks of terminals and computers, along with maxi, mini, and micro processing equipment, how to guard against fraud or breaches of informational security, and how to approach all the other problems having to do with access to information.

9.   THE COMPUTER IS "FILE ORIENTED"

Your complete system, the pure management system is an *action-oriented* plan. The computer's emphasis is on the record and on the file (made up of a number of related records). Thus we can say it tends to be a file-oriented machine. You will find that computers and computer people are preoccupied with the record and with the file. Various files "fold into libraries," and the total library can become a data base.

This heavy attention on the memory aspects of the system can be distracting if you are not alert. The key word in the management system is ACTION. Information kept on a record anywhere is memory—a secondary function. A record can be used to get action, but it is not action. The action itself is, of course, active behavior from people who react to the information carried on an action type of form.

Of course computers can and do turn out action forms such as requisitions, payroll checks, or invoices. And the computer can also let people read the record (memory of past actions and present status) on a terminal or on a printout device. Often somebody wants to know the status of a customer's account . . . or the status of an inventory item. "What is the balance today?" is a typical question.

So the processing activity around the computer pivots around a file . . . and the records within each file. If the file is on employees, one employee's record is the pivot. If it is around customers, a record on one customer is the pivot.

10. THE MEMBERS OF THE COMPUTER'S "FAMILY"

Let's look at the essential parts of a computer "family."

Data Processor The computer really is just one machine, the central processing unit (CPU or CP). It either does all the productive work, or it directs the "peripheral gear" that does some of the work. The CPU is the data processing brain. Yet it does nothing without specific instructions contained in a program. The program is the computer's "job outline."

The processor has a high-speed memory. This formerly was an array of magnetic cores, but today more of the characters are stored by using semiconductors, particularly metal-oxide semiconductor field-effect transistors (MOSFET).

In the minicomputer this high-speed memory can hold a limited number of characters, usually from 4000 to 64,000. In the largest computers, the high-speed memory (at very high cost) can run into the millions of characters. A character is a single letter (A to Z), a digit (0 to 9), or a punctuation mark. *Example:* IBM's 370/168 in one installation has 3,072,000 characters of storage. Software alone (operating systems) can use up to 100,000 character positions on the large computer. Then you need positions for the application program and for the data to be worked on, the transaction cluster.

You might as well try to count the stars as to list the character positions on very large equipment. And just as economists use the word "trillion," computer folks use words like megabyte . . . which non-technicians could express by saying, "an awful lot." And the memory can be expanded by a manipulation that the technicians call "virtual memory."

What is stored in this high-speed memory? Before the computer can go to work on the job of processing data, it brings in various types of data. First it brings in the information that represents the transaction. Then from its magnetic storage, it calls for the record (memory) that relates to that transaction. If the transaction is a new purchase by customer Smith, Mr. Smith's record must be brought in. In addition, the high-speed memory contains the application program that will update the memory (record) by adding, for example, the new purchase amount to the record. Also in the memory are operating programs that enable the machine to do its work. These are called *software*. Both application programs and operating programs (software) are really detailed instructions to the computer. Some analysts refer to these two types of instruction sets as:

1. Applications software . . . the instructions written to solve a specific "problem" (payroll, inventory, sales analysis)

2. Systems software . . . the operating system needed to control the jobs, and so on, that the hardware itself stops short of doing

Under the specific directions provided by the program, the CPU can compare two figures to see whether they are the same, or if one figure is greater or smaller. It can do arithmetic, perform simple forms of logic, and make *yes* or *no* decisions.

Will much calculating work be required in the new system? The CPU is a master calculator. It is also the director of other data manipulation activity. It can pull in data, either from the data entry (input) point or from magnetic storage. It can refile the data in the disk or tape storage, or it can issue a print-out for people to read.

In addition to the CPU, three other devices are required to do any electronic data processing:

1. Data ENTRY (input) devices
2. Data STORAGE devices
3. Data OUTPUT devices

Data Entry   Some analysts call data input "data encoding" . . . or just "encoding." Others prefer the term "data entry." To use the computer you need a way to put data into it. This is the data entry function. A worker can key in the information about a transaction by using keys similar to those on a typewriter and adding machine. Data can also be entered by punching a card and placing it in a reader that is connected to the CPU. (Most data used to enter the machine via the punched card, but this method of entry is fast declining in popularity.)

Other data entry devices include scanning by optical character recognition (OCR) equipment, through magnetic ink (MICR) and the required equipment (used for bank checks), and through electronic codes made up of thick and thin black lines (bar codes).

The bar codes * can be read by an optical scanning device such as are now appearing at retail food store checkout counters. Many articles in the retail grocery stores already carry the bar codes, even though the checkout devices are not yet installed. Look for them on cereal boxes.

The code on the side of freight cars (car numbers) can be read as the cars pass by a stationary electronic reader. Some cash registers are point-of-sale (POS) input devices. There are other entry means, but they are highly specialized.

* The "Universal Product Code."

All data enters or leaves the computer complex through the CPU. As information about a transaction comes in, it goes directly or indirectly into the CPU's high-speed memory; also stored in the high-speed memory is the program (set of instructions) that tells the CPU what to do with the data that comes in.

Storage   Since the computer is "file oriented," the electronic activity pivots around a record that is stored, not in the CPU's high-speed memory, but in magnetic storage on either disks, tapes, or drums. Such storage mediums cost less than the CPU's high-speed memory storage.

As the transaction data comes into the processor through any portal, the CPU goes to work, calls in the related record, updates it, and disposes of the developed data by sending that data back to storage. (In some cases it immediately prints out the data.)

In large systems the data cluster to be printed out is often sent to a temporary disk or tape storage before going through the printing process. (Spooling) In other cases the machine prints out the data at once.

The records on systems such as inventory, personnel, customers, or other types of files are stored in magnetic form in a CPU-connected storage medium . . . either tape or disk.

The records on a tape are stored sequentially—perhaps alphabetically in the case of personnel records, or by part numbers in the case of an inventory file. To retrieve each record from the tape and bring it into the central processing unit (or to provide information for someone at a terminal), the computer must search for that specific record in sequence. This is similar to the job of looking for a single frame on a long strip of movie film.

For most systems the more desirable type of storage is that which provides for "random access" to each record. (You can go directly to the record you want.) There are a number of other accessing techniques, but they tend to become more expensive per "look up" than sequential processing. This function used to be on a magnetic drum, but today it is usually on a rotating magnetic disk.

The disk drive is something like a jukebox record player with a number of "platters." The machine's platters are coated with magnetic material and are stacked one upon the other. They whirl around at about 2000 revolutions per minute. Over and under each disk are a number of read-write heads, similar to those used on tape records. The platters are usually in packs, like several phonograph records stacked one on top of the other. The name: disk pack.

At one time storage on magnetic tape was cheaper than storage on disk, but now this cost difference has all but disappeared. That's why the most popular storage device is the magnetic disk. The disk drive is the operating unit in a cabinet (like a phonograph) . . . while the disk pack is the recording medium (like a stack of records)

You often hear the terms *real-time* or *on-line*. It is easier to define them by first illustrating what they *don't* mean. *Example:* A production worker withdraws 20 parts of part number 6831, an item carried in inventory. He uses a stockroom requisition. Now if the stockroom people accumulated all withdrawals (all the requisitions) until the end of the day and then ran them over to the computer room for processing, the computer would not be working in real time . . . the transactions would not be on-line. Suppose that during the day you look at the record in the memory (whether stored magnetically or hand posted) and the record indicates that 300 items of part 6831 were in inventory: that figure does not reflect the real situation. In other words the 20-unit withdrawal has left only 280 units actually in stock, but the record has not yet been updated—it says "300". Thus there is a discrepancy between actual quantity in stock and the record that is supposed to reflect facts. Many times this temporary discrepancy is not important, and in such cases the processing and record updating can be done at night. At other times, when it is vital that the record and the actual situation always be in balance, the record must be changed instantaneously . . . such as in an airline reservation system. The airline system must be on-line or based on "real time."

Output   In smaller computer installations the input and output functions are provided within the same machine, such as a teletype "terminal." An operator types in the information as data entry, and the machine itself (on instructions from the CPU) types out other information . . . lists, reports, checks, invoices.

Output is usually a "hard copy" (typed data on paper). Sometimes the output is a displayed message on the face of an electronic tube. The initials CRT (cathode ray tube) are commonly used to refer to this type of output.

In an inventory system, if you have a customer on the phone and need to know how many of part 4836 are now in inventory, it would be adequate to have the answer appear on a tube. But if you want the computer to print out invoices for shipments, you need a hard copy device.

Some outputs go directly onto microfilm so people can read the data later on microfilm readers (COM).

The hard copy printout is an essential type of output device. The CRT may be useful, but it cannot serve alone. You can't, for example, mail a CRT tube to the customer to display the invoice.

Hard copy printing (typing) can be by single characters (as on a typewriter) or a line at a time (as on a large computer's line printer). The one-character-at-a-time printer is cheapest but slow. This is the type of printer used most often with minicomputers. Many operate in a speed range of 10 to 40 characters per second. (Some are faster.) The line printer is much faster but is often more costly than a minicomputer's CPU itself.

The word *memory* needs some explanation. In the early days of the computer, all the information in the computer complex was called memory, which it is. The information temporarily stored for processing in the CPU was called "high-speed memory," and data on tapes, disks, or in cards were stored in "low-speed memory." In computerese, the term *memory* now refers only to the metal-oxide semiconductor transistors or magnetic cores located in the CPU. All yield information at high speed . . . close to the speed of light.

Data stored on the computer's disks, on tapes, or in cards is now called data storage, or just plain *storage*.

11. RUNNING PAYROLL WITH THE SUPERCLERK

The computer can do routine jobs faster and more accurately than a clerk. However, most clerks *can* do the same work that the computer does. If you run a computer program for payroll, the machine can loop through the detailed instructions for processing payroll data for a thousand employees . . . and do it at the speed of light. It handles only the information relating to one employee at a time.

However the machine can only do part of the total systems job called "payroll." The result of a payroll system is payment for an employee's services, usually as a check (an action form). Subresults include a statement of earnings, a payroll journal, an employee earnings record . . . also ledgers on many deductions (putting money in other accounts) such as those for income taxes (state, city, and federal), union dues, contributions for social security and medical plans, insurance payments, credit union payments.

Let's look at the teamwork that takes place among clerical people and computer room workers in running a payroll system. We'll use the Playscript procedure format.

There, in a typical payroll system, you can see the normal identifiable system brackets . . . a trigger (the employee's time card) and the result (the employee's check).

Subject: Computer-assisted payroll system

Actor	Action
Employee	1. At the end of each day records time on form 387, TIME CARD.
	2. On the last work day of an employee's pay period, totals the number of hours worked on form 387, signs name in full, and places in "out" basket one hour before end of shift.
Department clerk	3. Picks up all completed time cards and takes to supervisor for approval.
	4. Retains approved cards at desk for time-keeping pickup.
Time clerk	5. Picks up time cards for employee groups at each department clerk's desk.
	6. Recalculates the total time per group to insure correctness. If there are errors, returns to individual supervisor for correction and initialing.
	7. Delivers all time cards to payroll clerk.
Payroll clerk	8. Enters all information needed for this pay period on computer form DP 1037, INPUT FORM.
	9. Calculates totals for each type of pay and posts such totals to form DP 1037, INPUT FORM.
	10. Delivers DP 1037 forms to computer center.
Computer control clerk	11. Logs in payroll input forms and sends to data entry (or encoding).
Key disk operator	12. Keys in variable information for each employee, checking the visual display for correctness. (In many cases the data processing manager requires the accuracy of

---

Between these two points we have a channel of action in which the following actors take part:

Employee   Computer center control clerk
Department clerk   Encoding department *
Time clerk   Computer operator
Payroll clerk

Actually the computer is also an actor, operating under the control of the computer operator and the payroll program. This is a typical batch computer

---

* The input function can be executed by key punch, CRT input, typing on a terminal, key-to-disk typing, scanning, and so on.

Subject: Computer-assisted payroll system

Actor	Action
	the data to be verified: one operator does the encoding and another reenters the information to verify the correctness.)
	13. Sends all payroll input information to computer room.
Computer operator	14. (in a small installation) Loads disk pack with correct computer program and runs payroll proof report. Posts run book.
	15. Sends payroll proof report to control clerk.
Control clerk	16. Checks proof report to make sure all information will be developed correctly. Corrects any errors.
	17. Notifies computer operator to run the payroll.
Computer operator	18. Submits job with current input data, runs complete payroll, producing checks and all by-product reports.
	19. Returns all documents to control clerk (sometimes these are kept in the encoding area and then returned).
Control clerk	20. Checks for completeness, sorts by department, and logs out forms.
	21. Returns all documents to payroll clerk.
Payroll clerk	22. Picks up payroll documents from control clerk and re-checks for completeness.
	23. Places payroll checks in individual window envelopes, sorts by department, and delivers to department clerks.
Department clerk	24. Delivers checks to employees in the department.
	25. Sorts all reports and supplementary information by type in preparation for distribution.

operation in which the computer itself does an excellent job of handling the routine (mule work) required to produce a payroll.

From the user's viewpoint, there are only two important considerations . . . the input (the hours, information about the employee, totals, etc.) must be correct, and the outputs (checks and reports) must be correct and received on time.

Notice that at step 3 there is an implied actor . . . the supervisor who approves employees' time cards. Also, between steps 11 and 12 there is another implied actor, a data entry supervisor who assigns the keying-in jobs to the various operators.

In the sequence step 18, the computer (actually the processor) takes part as an actor. Using the master record that is now "read into" storage, the CPU matches the incoming time information against each employee's pay rate and updates the employee's earnings record.

Later, using the processed data, the computer can run subsidiary ledgers or records, overtime reports, a payroll journal, and so on.

12. PROGRAMMING LANGUAGES

The computer can't read our English letters or our arabic numbers. It uses a machine language, a rather moronic numbers language (binary) that is made up of eight columns; either a zero (0) or a one (1) appears in each column.

Thus data going into the computer or out of it must be interpreted from people language to machine language. In bringing out information, the computer changes its language into a people-readable language.

Whether the in-going string of data is from a time card (as in a payroll system) or as instructions in a small but complete 500-step applications program . . . the information must be translated into binary before the computer can use it.

Instructions for the computer are written in a special language that is close to English but is not quite the same. Programmers learn one of these languages and write the computer's instructions in it. Widely used programming languages are PL-1, RPG-II, COBOL, BASIC, and FORTRAN. Each of these must be converted by a special type of interpretive program called a compiler. (These interpretation problems are of minor concern to the systems user.)

The best known and probably widest used programming language is COBOL (Common Business-Oriented Language). Use of RPG-II (report program generator) is now increasing.

Why were these artificial languages developed? Because it was difficult for people to write programs in the computer's language . . . in binary.

When a programmer develops a new program which he will write in FORTRAN, COBOL, RPG-II, or some other widely used language, he goes through the following steps:

1. He states the problem or the situation.
2. He makes a flow chart that depicts the logic of the handling sequence for processing the information.
3. He codes the instructions on a programming form.
4. He (or a key encoding operator) either punches in this information or types it on a terminal's keyboard.
5. He runs the program in the programming language against the compiler program to get a machine-readable program.

Each programming language uses our alphabet and numbers and generally has from 45 to 50 characters. It includes the 26 letters of the English alphabet, the 10 numerical digits (0 through 9), and the special characters such as decimal points, dollar signs, slash marks, and parentheses.

13. INVENTORY: EVERYBODY'S SYSTEM

Can a computer make a contribution to the operation of an inventory system? Please recognize that inventory is often linked with other systems, particularly with order processing systems or with production systems. Nonetheless, the inventory system cycle can be isolated to serve its one specific purpose. The major result of any inventory system is:

> to supply the parts or materials needed to fill customers' orders, whether those customers are "in the house" or on the outside.

We can quickly break down the broad objective of the inventory system into these subresults, which are also essential:

1. Materials or stocks are always available *when* they are needed.
2. There are not more than needed.
3. There are not less than needed.
4. Materials "move" in and out rapidly; thus by increasing turnover, a reduction is achieved in capital invested in the inventory of parts or materials.

In an inventory system the major action form is one that permits people to *withdraw* stock. It may be a stockroom requisition, an order from a customer, or in any other form that results in a withdrawal. The major inventory action of withdrawal is, as usual, related to fulfilling the needs of people . . . either production people or customers.

Second in importance only to the withdrawal action is the replacement action. Reorders are necessary to maintain the stock at a minimum level so that the supply will not run out and will indeed "always be available when needed."

To put it in simple English, the inventory system is an activity first of put and take; then it becomes a question of "what is left?"

Systems planning for inventory recognizes that there are a number of different, identifiable costs in connection with the inventory function. These include:

1. The cost of *ordering* new supplies
2. The *actual cost* of the parts, materials, or items (what you pay the vendor)
3. The *transportation* cost coming from the vendor
4. *Receiving* costs
5. *Inspection* and checking costs
6. Materials *handling* costs
7. Costs of *storing* the materials
8. Cost of *issuing* the materials
9. The cost of *recording* the issuance or receipt of materials
10. Cost of the *investment* (capital)

Typically, in an inventory system, there are numerous related clusters of data, starting with the withdrawal data cluster. Here is how these clusters act and react in a system using the familiar functions of the system . . . action, memory, and report:

Work Functions	*Systems Functions*
1. Withdrawing items from inventory	Action
2. Processing by subtracting the quantity withdrawn to get a new balance	Memory
3. Is it time to reorder?	Memory and control
4. Ordering replacements	Action
5. Receiving the replacements	Action
6. Inspecting the replacements	Action
7. Placing replacements in stock	Action
8. Processing by adding to the record, getting a new balance	Memory and control
9. Fast-moving versus slow-moving stocks	Report
10. Setting minimum and maximum balance points on each item or article	Sets limits for control or a stage for action
11. Usage trends by specific items in inventory	Analytical report
12. Sales or usage forecasts	Set stage for possible action and for future reports
13. How many items of each on hand now?	Systems memory
14. Analyzing the sales by product categories	Reports
15. Relative profitability of products	Reports
16. Total dollar value of the inventory at one specific time, such as the first of the month.	Report

14. DECISION AIDS

Information taken from the records on inventory can become inputs to management people for making decisions. Here are some of the questions that executives ask before making decisions about inventory:

1. Shall we cut out the slow-moving stock or items? (Or is keeping them a worthwhile customer accommodation?)
2. Who are our largest customers? What do they buy?
3. Who are the smallest customers?
4. Where is our highest profitability?
5. Where do we incur most losses? On what items?
6. Shall we put in new items? What are the risks?
7. Shall we increase the quantity in inventory (boost the minimums and maximums)?
8. Shall we decrease the quantity of an item in inventory (lower the minimums and maximums)?
9. Are we achieving a balance line of sales?
10. Shall we change the monetary incentives for salesmen?
11. Shall we take steps to sell more of the most profitable items?
12. How often are there stock-outs?
13. How many back orders? What is the total dollar value?
14. Are the inventory turnovers satisfactory?

15. COMPUTER–GENERATED REPORTS

It is the system's transaction that gathers data. Once the transaction is complete and the systems result has been obtained, the data has no more value from an action/transactional viewpoint. But such dead data has an important residual value, not for action, but as an aid to the man or woman who must review the *results* of the action.

In Chapter 9, DESIGNING THE NEW SYSTEM, we said that systems reports should be a part of the systems plan . . . not an afterthought as many reports are. Robert Shultis points out:

Although the action part of the system is important, management usually judges a system by the reports it gets or doesn't get.

There are many types of special reports. Our concern here is with a routine type of report: the *systems report*.

Caution: Don't think you can impress the manager by presenting him with pounds of paper carrying detailed data that he has no time to read. And if he found the time, the glut of data wouldn't mean anything to him. An "activity recital" is usually a waste of computer and printout time. It won't waste a manager's time. He won't read it. And he won't feel any respect for the analyst who doesn't really know what a systems report is.

If a manager can get accurate, timely information on any facet of the business, he can make sound decisions. If the computer provides such information, the manager is going to feel kindly toward data processing people.

The first type of information an operating manager needs is a report on results. His people get results by doing work—work that is performed within a segment of a systems channel . . . even if the employees are not aware of any such phenomenon as a system.

Your report must be a by-product of the systems action, not a patch-on, subsystem designed only to produce a report. A systems report tells a manager:

1. The result is LESS than it should be.

    or

2. The result is JUST what it should be.

    or

3. The result is MORE than it should be.

To be useful, a systems report must report against a specific plan or standard. If it is a report on performance in the shipping department, the manager who reads that report must be aware of a definite standard.

For an example, let's reconsider (we did it first in Chapter 9) the shipping system. Here's a standard: A shipping staff of 7 persons can handle and dispatch an average of 52 shipments in an 8-hour shift. Fifty-two is the output standard.

If a document merely says, "The shipments on April 24th totaled 43," it isn't a report at all. If it just lists all the shipments made, it is merely an activity recital.

To make that report of real value, the analyst must design it so that it includes what the results *should be*. To spew out dozens of activity recitals on a computer's printer is simply busy work. And just calling such an output a "report" doesn't make it a report.

Whether a systems report is generated by the computer or by hand, the same six essentials are required. We reviewed these essentials in Chapter 9, but since they are so vital to good reporting, let's consider them again.

1. THE SUBJECT. What does the report cover? *Example:* "Total sales for the Spokane territory."
2. The EXACT PERIOD covered by the report. Don't say "for the week of November 7th." Do say "from November 7th through November 13th."
3. The DATE the report is ISSUED. This must be within a day or two of the end date of the period covered. (Slow feedback is about as valuable as last week's newspaper.)
4. PLANNED RESULTS or the standard (which really is a plan). This must be specific . . . 16 engineering changes released using 280 man-hours.
5. ACTUAL RESULTS. Again, be *specific:* 15 engineering changes released, using 310 man-hours.
6. THE DIFFERENCE. Under plan? Over plan? Is there a tolerance? If the planned result was 16 and the actual result was 15, would the chief engineer (the manager) consider the result tolerable? The man-hours used were 30 more than planned and the results were 15, not 16 releases. Would these facts stir up the chief enough to make him want to discuss the results with his project engineers?

If a manager gets a report that contains those six essential facts on the performance of the work for which he is responsible, he can control the work action by either of two decisions, as follows:

1. If the actual performance is reasonably equal to the planned performance, he does nothing. (Doing nothing represents a decision not to take action.)
2. If the actual performance is substantially at variance with the plan, he can:
   a. redirect the action to get it back on the planned track
   b. change the plan itself

Note: It is foolish to send a systems report to any person who does not have the authority to redirect the action or to change the plan.

What are examples of systems reports that can be computer generated by using the residual information taken from completed transactions? Consider:

1. Reports on sales by customer
2. Reports on sales by products
3. Reports on sales by sales territory
4. Reports on commissions of salesmen and agents

5. Reports on inventory standings
6. Order backlog reports
7. Back order reports by total dollar volume
8. Reports on cost of sales by product and by percent of margin
9. Reports on overtime
10. Reports on accounts receivable collections and on open accounts and their ages
11. Reports of shipments by warehouses

16. COMPUTER ACTION ON AN INVENTORY

What happens when the information about a withdrawal from inventory reaches the CPU? Consider this little dramatic sequence, occurring when the withdrawal transaction data cluster enters the processor. Technically the action doesn't go exactly as described, but the following is essentially accurate.

Actor	Action
Withdrawal data cluster (a transaction)	1. Hello, here I am, ready to be worked on.
Computer (CPU)	2. What kind of transaction are you?
Withdrawal data cluster	3. Look at my transaction code. I represent a withdrawal transaction. John Jones took 42 parts of model 3786 from the stockroom to work on at his bench.
Computer (processor)	4. Okay, you're in. (To storage.) Hey, you. Send in a master record, the one on the inventory status of model 3786.
Disk storage	5. Yes, master. Here is the record on 3786. (It is pulsing its way into the processor's high-speed memory. There it occupies a number of character positions.)
Computer	6. (Scratching his computer-head memory.) Let me see. The withdrawal is for 42 parts of model 3786. I'll subtract that from 851, the last balance on the record.
	7. This gives a new balance of 809. I'll erase the 851 on the record and put 809 in its place. That is the new balance.
	8. Oh, yes, I'd also better check that reorder point against the new balance, too.
	9. Oh, here it is. The reorder point is 500 of the part. Is that less than 809? (A little subtraction goes on here in the high-speed memory.) Yes, it is less, so I don't need to order more of model 3786 this time.

Actor	*Action*
	10. Back to storage with you, record 3786. Disk storage, put this record back into the inventory file at the same location (address).
Disk storage	11. Will do, master.
Computer	12. Well, I guess I'd better look around again. Here comes another withdrawal transaction in through the door. It has a different number. Here we go again. Who are you? What is *your* transaction code?
	13. Storage, send over the inventory record for model 6261 . . .

17. WHAT WORK NEEDS TO BE DONE?

You know your new system from trigger to result and all its subsystems. OK. What work must be done? You know. Write it down. Then you can ask the following questions: Can a computer help? Can it make a contribution that also makes sense economically? Will the cost be less than the value?

You designed the new system purely as a management system. You were not hung up on computers, typewriters, pencils, or manifolding form sets. Your question was always: What is the best way to get *this* work done?

Typical types of work required by a system include these samples.

1. Filing information for later use (systems memory).
2. Do arithmetic . . . add, subtract, divide, or multiply.
3. Write.
4. Read.
5. Compare.
6. Sort.
7. Update a file record.
8. Provide information for a worker who has a need to know (printed on an action form or, if a record, displayed on a tube face).
9. Provide an executive with knowledge on results or lack of them (report).
10. Summarize information, boiling it down and making it available for people who must make a high-level decision.
11. Providing information gathered by different categories . . . for a manager's analysis.

18. WORK CAUSED BECAUSE
YOU USE THE COMPUTER

Let's remember the old breakdown principle that applies to any type of work. All work can be divided into these identifiable stages:

1. Getting ready to work
2. Working
3. Cleaning up after working

The only productive stage is number 2 . . . *working*. To increase the output of work, you first concentrate on ways to reduce the first and third stages, to get them as close to zero as possible.

Then you give your attention to the working stage itself, analyzing it to see how it can be simplified and made more productive. This three-stage approach to increase results can be highly effective, often increasing total productivity from 20 to 60%.

In the light of these three stages of work, recognize that the computer also must do (1) get-ready work and (2) clean-up work. The computer is only productive when it is doing exactly what you know must be done in the system . . . arithmetic, record updating, filing records, retrieving records, printing out or displaying data, sorting, summarizing.

Those functions are worth dollars to your organization. But what about coding, programming, data entry punching, language selection, software purchases, compiling, assembling, editing, checking? How much are these "entry" efforts worth to the system? That's right: *Nothing*. They represent a cost you must bear just because YOU ARE USING THE COMPUTER!

How about the other functions, including the activity we call output? How much are these activities worth to your system: forms decollation (taking out the carbons), bursting, sorting, . . . modem operations, transmission line, rentals, library activities (storage for disk packs, tapes, and cards), computer-run schedules, power backup, security measures? How about preventive maintenance and service contract costs?

What the computer does for your system at the second stage—at the working stage—has to be so valuable that it more than offsets the costs you incur just because you are *using* the computer!

19. THE SCALE OF BUSINESS

No question about it. Many organizations today could not operate on the present scale if the computer had not come along.

As an example, the scale on which we operate our airline reservation systems would be impossible today if we were using clerks as we did 20 years ago. In Chapter 2 we indicated that banking couldn't operate as it now does without the computer, using a remark of an executive of the Bank of America. Let's paraphrase it here:

> If we weren't using electronic data processing to help us with our book-
> keeping and our systems, we would have to use every adult in California
> to serve as clerks and accountants just for our operations.

Can the computer make a contribution to *your* system? Will it "pay" more than it "costs"? Only you can judge.

You know that system from end to end. You know the trigger and the result. You know the channels and the side channels, the connections and the interconnections.

When you design the system without thinking of a computer or any other tool—when you design a "pure" management system—you'll know exactly what work must be done to execute the transactions that will flow through that system.

So whether you use a computer or you don't . . . whether you use brand A or B or C . . . the answer will depend on how straight you think. If you faithfully follow the classic path to systems improvement, the answer to the use of any tool will be reasonably easy.

When the manager uses the computer as a tool, not as a substitute for his own thinking, it can bring forth facts he can use in making a decision. He can use the information provided by the machine as a guide when he has to make decisions.

Furthermore, he can use the machine to monitor a present system's results. Is the system getting the right results? Are the costs right? Is the quality right?

He can use the computer to develop early warning signals in relation to his operation. Then he can take decisive action *before* disaster is upon him. He can use the machine to help him to serve as a more effective steward of his organization's resources.

And if he sees that there is a mountain of clerical work to be done in his department, he can whistle for the superclerk.

ARE THERE ANY
USEFUL SYSTEMS PRINCIPLES?

Pareto's Law   In the 1800's Vilfredo Pareto, an Italian economist, studied the distribution of wealth and income in Italy. Conclusions from his research are expressed in Pareto's law:

> For any series of elements that are to be controlled, a certain small fraction in terms of numbers of elements, always accounts for the major portion in terms of effect.

Men and women who design inventory systems find, in this law, an aid to their own thinking. *Example:* An analyst may discover that out of 50,000 different items in an inventory, only 5000 account for 80% of the total *value* of the inventory. Thus using Pareto's law, any large group of elements can be broken down into the vital few and the trivial many.

Question: Is that statement a *law?* Or a *hypothesis,* or a *principle,* or a *theory?*

The statement is certainly an aid to the thinking of professional people . . . managers and analysts. *Another example:* One company issued a policy on employee absenteeism requiring a doctor's certificate for any absence of more than two days. On analyzing *who* was absent, the personnel manager found that only a small percentage of all employees accounted for most of the absences. Thereupon the company revised the policy to require a doctor's certificate for any unexcused absence in excess of 5 days that accumulated during the previous 12 months. Thus the policy was changed to require medical certification only for the individuals who were the main cause of the absenteeism problem.

A few years ago we wondered how widely applicable were the systems principles and theories that we had discovered during our working years. So we invited 21 prominent educators and top systems practitioners from across the nation to work with us to solidify the principles that we offered and to suggest others that they had found useful.

What is a theory? What is a principle? During the two-day workshop the registrants were also asked to offer terms that could be synonyms for the word *principle*. They offered the following list of could-be synonyms.

1. Hypothesis
2. Principle
3. Theory
4. Law
5. Concept
6. Precept
7. Postulate
8. Abstraction
9. Fundamental
10. Proposition

1. ARE PRINCIPLES USED IN CONSULTING?

In any organization you find people using specialized methods of working that outsiders could not know. These are the "practices" of that specific business or trade. The one practice that all organizations have in common is financial accounting, but even here the exact accounting practices vary.

How is it then, that a management consultant can advise managers who operate in different types of organizations? Obviously he cannot know the specific work practices of the people doing the work of different clients. He couldn't possibly be as expert in such knowledge as the practitioners. True, there are some specialty consultants. Our reference pertains to *management* consultants.

Such an individual can move from one organization to another and provide a useful advisory service to each. He can do so even if he does not know the different businesses from a technical viewpoint.

We can only conclude that he uses principles . . . theories . . . or laws. These guide his thinking. He is able to apply such principles to any organization regardless of its technical aspects,

What are the mysterious keys that can open the door to improvement in any organization? After our own years of practice in the systems and management field, we concluded that certain systems principles do exist. The problem first is to discover them. Then the job is to state them so that we can teach them to others. We must be able to pass them on to people coming into systems improvement work. Only in this way can a true systems profession develop. Nobody invents principles . . . people (who both work AND think) discover them.

2. UNIVERSAL APPLICATION IS ESSENTIAL

If your principle is truly such, whether you call it a hypothesis or a theory or a law, it must be universally applicable.

1. It must apply to any *system* such as purchasing, inventory, personnel, or law enforcement.
2. It must apply to any *type of organization* . . . government, industry, financial, retail, military, or educational.
3. It must apply to any *size* of organization . . . whether 2 people or 200,000 people.
4. The principle must be just as useful in designing a *manual* system as it is when the analyst is working on a *computer-* based system.

3. REQUIREMENTS OF THE STATEMENTS

To be useful, the statement cannot be vague or up in the air. It must mean something to a person who is working in the field. It must cause him to think conceptually.

How useful is the statement of a principle in *teaching* systems? That is the real test. If the statement of the principle cannot be used to teach, or if it is meaningless when taught to the students of systems improvement work, the statement is not yet in useful form. (This "useful form" is meaningful only to a practicing systems analyst. It would mean nothing to someone not in systems work.)

The novice in systems work can start by applying a small number of selected systems principles. Three or four would be enough for a starter. Since this distillation of experience came to the old timers the hard way, the new person benefits from past effort. The principle is there to guide him (1) to success and (2) equally to help him avoid common mistakes. Then he doesn't depend entirely on his own experience and his personal trial-and-error practice.

Each statement of principle should be interesting enough and short enough to allow the student to memorize it.

Successful practitioners constantly use theory and principles in their work. So do consultants. But because the concepts are not expressed and never written, they are largely unteachable. Therefore their value begins and ends with a single individual. A profession can hardly advance when each new practitioner must learn the hard way (trial and error) what his predecessors have already learned.

The statement of principle has value only when it enables a practitioner to move more rapidly and more surely to a successful result when he designs a new system.

Now let's look at a number of statements of systems principles. They all have been useful. They are universally applicable. They can be applied to any size or any type of organization and to any system operating within that organization.

Principle No. 1. Provide First for the "Main Line"

Out of any total quantity of systems transactions, a large percentage will require specific steps of processing in order to reach the result. This path of the majority of transactions, this channel, is the system's "main line." You can identify the main line of a system either by the great quantity of transactions or by the relatively greater importance of such transactions.

Along any systems main line there are also sidetracks. These are exceptions and variations. As a designer, consider how to handle the latter only after you have specified the path of the main line flow of work. Over such a main line the normal transactions can move rapidly, without hindrance.

By thinking of the system's main line, the analyst will not be tempted to put all transactions through the unusual or greater number of processing steps required by a minority of transactions.

Example: If 90% of the transactions can go through the systems channel in 10 processing steps, and the remaining 10% can be completed in 11 to 25 work steps, do not make the "easy" 90% go through steps 11 to 25.

Only after you have designed the main line for a straight through flow of most transactions (most directly from the trigger to the result), do you provide for the necessary sidetracks . . . for the variations and exceptions.

At each point where an exception or variation could be discovered, make it clear to the operator at that station how he or she can identify that variation. Then the operator can switch such transactions from the main line and onto a sidetrack for special handling.

Principle No. 2. People Participation

To be highly useful, a system cannot be designed by a professional analyst working alone. Nothing solo. The analyst must be joined by the people who are involved in processing information provided by that system.

Wherever people are running a system, the analyst must apply the principle of participation. The systems user, the man or woman who will operate the new system, must take part in the design of that system. The user's role may be a minor one. It tends to center on a better way to do work at that person's work station.

Operators are systems users who do the work required to complete a transaction. They have an expert's knowledge of the work executed at their specific work stations.

The "give and take" of true participation between the user and the analyst/designer will result in the development of a new system that is both better and is accepted by the user.

Improvement suggestions offered by operating people are usually practical ones. Because they have been consulted on coming changes, they tend to accept the new system when it is installed. Resistance to change is minimized.

Participation takes place at all stages in a systems development project. This includes survey, analysis, design, rechecking, installation, and follow-up.

Principle No. 3. Selecting a Logical Systems Cycle

Within any organization there is a network of systems that seem to be intertwined, tangled, and interconnected. The layman rarely identifies these many activities as specific, modular systems. But the analyst, in order to improve one system quickly, isolates one segment of the activities into a "logical package" of teamwork. We call this a logical systems cycle. Each logical systems cycle is enclosed by two identifiable brackets: (1) a transactional *trigger* and (2) the *result* of the activity. In the execution of a specific systems function, people skills in various departments are connected and form a (invisible) systems team.

An organization chart is a "vertical view" of the organization structure. A system is a "horizontal view" of that organization's action-getting structure.

These channels of systems action often run across department boundaries. They tend to tie together the work, the individual efforts of the people "residing" in those departments.

A logical cycle is a systems module that is not too small nor too large. If its redesign could be done in a day, it is probably too small. If its redesign would take more than six months of study, redesign, and installation work . . . it is probably too large.

The cycle starts when the transaction is launched at the "trigger point." There will follow a series of processing steps, work necessary to carry the transaction along to reach the result. The selection of the systems cycle is neither a science nor a technique. It is an art.

Example: In an activity known as *purchasing* the logical cycle would include these broad steps:

1. Recognizing a need for materials or supplies
2. Launching an action form to fill that need
3. Receiving the article or services
4. Paying the bill for same

In a very large purchasing system (high volume of transactions) the total procurement activity could be divided into two or more cycles such as: (1) the replacement of stock as one cycle and (2) the money settlement (accounts payable), as a related but separate cycle.

Principle No. 4. The Three Systems Functions

The three essential functions of a management system are:

1. The ACTION function
2. The MEMORY function
3. The REPORTING function

Action   The system has only one basic reason for existing: that is, TO GET A RESULT. This result is one that only a *group* of people, working as a team, could achieve. Therefore the management system is "action and work oriented." Data and data processing are means, not ends. Usually people get this action by issuing an action form such as an order.

Systems Memory The data generated as an aftermath of getting the action is a by-product of the system's energy, and such data can be used to establish memory and provide reports. These subresults of the action enable managers to exercise control over the action.

The most common example of the system's memory is a record, such as a record of a customer, a record of an employee, a record relating to a client, or a record that reflects the quantity status of one item in inventory.

These records are not dynamic in themselves. They are reflections of the action (transaction) side of the system. Sometimes a record consists of an extra copy of an action form but is used for a memory function.

In addition to establishing data recall that relates to transactions, the memory also provides for the reuse of information. *Example:* Items such as a customer's number, name, and address, need not be written each time if they have been stored in the system's memory. They can be reused when the same customer is involved in another transaction.

Systems Report The third function of the management system is reporting. A systems report is a cluster of information about the results of the action (usually springing out of the system's memory). A report goes to a man or woman who is responsible for looking at results of the action and comparing the results against an acceptable standard.

This person must know what the results from action *should be!* If the report

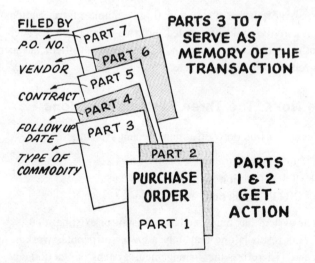

The same data cluster used to get action can also serve as a systems memory. The data are identical, but the systems function is different.

to such a person indicates that results are not what they should be, it is up to this individual to do one of two things:

1. Redirect that action and put it back on the track.
2. Change the plan or reset the standard.

The person who evaluates performance on the basis of the report supplied to him by the system asks questions such as:

Did the people get this result *on time?*
Did they get the *result* that the action should get?
Was the *quality* of the result satisfactory?
Was the *cost* of getting the result higher or lower than standard?

Principle No. 5. Identifying the "Big Show"

Any organization has at least one major reason for existing. Identify it. Write it out. Are there several "big shows" in your organization? Name them. Write a short description of each.

If the systems analyst concentrates on systems directly affecting the "big show" of his organization, those efforts can produce the greatest benefits in the shortest time. Second, by recognizing that other activities are support activities, the analyst will tend to develop other systems as supports, not as ends in themselves. All systems must contribute to the execution of the primary activities of the organization.

The big show of a specific organization could be law enforcement, money lending and borrowing, manufacturing, designing, selling, serving members, or serving clients successfully.

Profit is *not* a big show activity. It is a by-product of doing the big show work well. Profit is also a safety valve ensuring that the outgo of funds does not exceed the income, permitting the organization to continue to serve its big show purpose. Profit also helps to secure more capital by providing dividends for those who will lend to or invest their money in the organization.

Principle No. 6. Exceptions and Variations

Exceptions and variations might be considered side systems or sidetracks. The main line will either carry the bulk of these activities through a minimum number of processing steps . . . or it will carry the most important transactions. But other transactions will come under the category of variations or exceptions.

A transaction *variation* will "run" partially but not entirely on the main line. It may run partially on it and at certain process points require a sidetrack. Here it will receive extra processing or different processing needed for the completion of that unusual transaction. Most variations are known at the time the analyst and the users design the new system. So the designers provide for the handling of known variations. The first prerequisite for designing a sidetrack is to help an operating person (at one work station) to identify such a transaction AS a variable transaction.

Exceptions are the transactions that are not covered by the main line nor by the sidetracks that are designed as part of the system. Therefore exceptions require individual, human attention. They cannot be handled by routine processing. An exception may only occur once in a hundred times or once in five thousand times. It is not economically feasible to set up a sidetrack system for such rare transactions. Exceptions are nonroutine. Neither the main line nor any systems sidetrack can provide adequately for their occurrence.

The exception, like the variation, must be identified by an operating person.

Principle No. 7. Direct Result

Shorten the channel between the trigger and the result of the system by asking, "How can we reach that result with a minimum of work steps along the channel?" The ideal would be to go directly from the trigger to the result with no processing between.

Principle No. 8. Providing Latitude for Individual Initiative

Provide, in the systems plan, for a channel that goes as directly as possible from trigger to result. Leave the development of detailed job outlines or work instructions to supervisors and to their workers.

Although each individual who takes part in the team play called a management system must play his role well and must work in coordination with others, it is desirable to leave reasonable latitude for the exercise of individual initiative where possible. But such initiative must be exercised *within* the limits of the team play.

4. AUTHORITATIVE OBSERVATIONS ON THEORY

The following selections are quotations by various authorities relating to principles and theories.

Karl von Klausewitz, German military writer/strategist:
The first business of every theory is to clear up conceptions and ideas which have become jumbled together and, we may say, entangled and confused.

Ian Hamilton, English military strategist:
When they first meet with analysis applied to the task of management, many managers feel embarrassed. They tell themselves that they are practical men and that theory is of no value anyway.

Lyndall Urwick, British consultant:
Theory is lightfooted. It can adapt itself to changed circumstances, think out fresh combinations and can peer into the future.
(On the other hand), faced with new and unaccustomed situations, practice can only explore it tentatively . . . by trial and error.

Henri Fayol, French industrialist and student of management (to his newly hired engineers who were management trainees):
The theoretical knowledge which you possess will permit you to assimilate quickly all details of any kind whatsoever.
Without principles one is in darkness and chaos. Interest, experience, and proportion are still handicapped even with the best principles.
The principle is the lighthouse fixing the bearings. But it can only serve those who already know the way into the port.

Harold Koontz, American professor of management:
There's a question in my mind as to whether enough attention has been given to the development of a conceptual framework of principles from which to approach the problem of improving management.
It appears that much of the research being undertaken, and much of the effort to train managers, has been proceeding from a questionable premise: *That exchanges of experience, with emphasis on techniques, are a means for attacking the problem.*

George W. Troost, vice-president of Chrysler (in 1955): There is no end to the demand for men who can see the simple pattern in a mass of detail; who can see the possibility of order in apparent chaos . . .

5. CHARACTERISTICS OF A GREAT MANAGEMENT SYSTEM

How can you know whether you have a so-so system or a really good one? Or even a great one? About the only way you could grade a phenomenon as intangible as a system is by the characteristics that it manifests. And even some of these characteristics may be difficult to determine. But let's try anyway. Here are some of the characteristics of a superior system.

1. It does work.
2. It gets results.
3. It has an acceptable * time span for transactions that go through the channel.
4. The action data clusters convey the work message to each person who needs it . . . quickly and accurately.
5. The memory data clusters are arranged for easy manipulation and for significant readouts to people who need to know the current status of a subject or a set of transactions.
6. Summarization by any category is easy.
7. The work required to process a transaction flows along smoothly.
8. No errors go through, or they are caught early and corrected.
9. The operating staff, the systems users, are well trained.
10. All nonsystems obstacles are removed. *Examples:* Wrong policy, lack of air conditioning, poor lighting, poor organization structure, unfavorable working conditions, and an unplanned layout.
11. People with the necessary skills are on the right job, and they understand how to do that job.
12. A minimum of data flows through the system's channel.
13. The distance from the trigger to the result is relatively short.
14. The people who use the system not only accept it but really like it and enjoy working with it.
15. Every person gets the data he needs:
    a. only in the form he wants
    b. on time
    c. accurately
16. There is no excess paperwork.
17. The system doesn't try to handle a nonroutine transaction (an exception) on a routine basis.

* Speed versus cost. There must be a compromise. Too much speed usually costs too much.

18. It uses the most simple machines and least expensive equipment. Each tool makes a contribution of value that outweighs its cost.
19. It is responsive to people's needs for information. They never have to dig, scrounge, or go without information.
20. The action is under control at all times. If it doesn't go as planned, this fact will come quickly to the attention of a person who has the power to redirect the action.
21. Involved executives and supervisors are not burdened by routine detail. They can give their attention to activities that only they could handle.
22. People at the operating level can run the system without direct supervision.
23. It doesn't try to do jobs that no management system can do.
24. It is modular and flexible. Parts of it are easy to change as the action requirements change.
25. It identifies and provides for the handling of variations and exceptions.

CHAPTER 14

THE ANALYST AND
THE SYSTEMS USER

1. Sources of systems analysts
2. Characteristics of an analyst
3. The technical tidal wave
4. The language barrier
5. Training
6. Leadership opportunity
7. Who are systems users?
8. The fear of a little knowledge
9. What should the user know?

In the days when people designed only manual systems, such as the 1930's, 1940's, and 1950's, systems analysts and systems users worked together. Much of such early systems improvement work pivoted around the procedure.

The manager of a department may have found that some aspect of a system wasn't working as it should, at least not in his department. He requested a change to that system by revising a portion of the procedure. (Each major system was reflected by a procedure.)

Then the analyst checked out the proposed change with other department chiefs. If all agreed that the change was desirable or that it would not adversely affect another department, the analyst issued a new procedure to reflect the revision.

During that period the punched card (unit record) tabulating machine was available, but it was used primarily for accounting functions. The early name for such equipment was "electric accounting machine." (EAM).

Most early systems functions were located in accounting departments and were referred to as SYSTEMS and PROCEDURES. As the use of automatic equipment started to grow, particularly in the mid-1950's, other department chiefs began to resent efficiency experts from accounting "nosing around" in their departments.

Gradually the systems and data processing function moved to a more acceptable position in the organization . . . that of administration.

1. SOURCES OF SYSTEMS ANALYSTS

Formerly an analyst had an accounting or an industrial engineering background. He (there were almost no women in the field before 1955) may or may not have had a college degree. In 1958 we took a census of analysts in the Los Angeles area. Of 724 practicing systems analysts only 9 were women . . . about 1.25%. Five of those lady "systems men" worked for government agencies.

Women analysts today, mostly coming from the ranks of programmers, probably account for about 10% of all people doing systems analysis. But the proportion of women to men is growing.

Where do capable analysts come from? What education do they have? In what college subjects did they specialize? Most have bachelor's degrees and about 20% have received graduate degrees, usually an MBA (master of business administration). Computer science subjects are their major courses.

Many large corporations bring in one or more crops of trainees each year. The training period is usually from six weeks to six months and then the new people are ready to go to work. Some promising employees from operating departments may enter the training program as a part of one of the yearly "crops." A small percentage of experienced analysts come from other firms.

One corporation using 550 analysts, trains from 70 to 90 new analysts/programmers a year. Another, with 150 analysts and 200 programmers (in this case the two functions are not combined), trains from 40 to 50 new people a year. Most newcomers go from training into the programmer ranks. After two or three years of experience in programming, some individuals emerge as full-fledged analysts. Their experience in working with the computer and its related gear gives them an excellent base for analysis work.

Within today's computer-related systems activities, there are at least four general groups of people:

1. Systems analysts
2. Programmers
3. Computer operators, including data entry personnel
4. Support people . . . librarians, maintenance personnel, clerks, secretaries, training specialists, documentation people

The trainee crop may include promising people from computer operations or from the computer support areas. In some organizations the analyst is capable of programming his own system.

Some experienced analysts come from consulting firms, from software suppliers, and from computer manufacturing companies. Still others learned how to program or to perform systems analysis during their military service.

2. CHARACTERISTICS OF AN ANALYST

If a man can't analyze, he can't make it as an analyst. This is true to a large extent of the programmer. He needs analytical ability, too.

Both analysts and programmers are problem solvers. The problem is how to design a better system and put it to work. To do that job the ability to analyze is essential. I've found that I couldn't use some very intelligent men and women on my systems staff because they were not able to ask penetrating questions.

Yet the analyst must ask his questions in a quiet, humble way, or he makes a mess of the human relations side. Operating people respect smart analysts; they resent smartie analysts. And operating people who don't like an analyst probably won't like his system.

Even if he isn't particularly fond of people, the real "pro" among the many analysts recognizes that people who run the system are the most important ingredient in a good system. I've seen several eager analysts, capable and intelligent people, who failed to produce good systems until they realized that such a production must be a team effort, not a one-man show.

One analyst, a former industrial engineer, created a furor among the operating people (the systems users). He had pushed through a new computer system in record time (three months). His boss was about to fire or transfer him. The systems users, including people with political clout, were after his scalp. The users referred to him as "that arrogant analyst."

Yet the man was intelligent, experienced, and a driver. His technical design was outstanding. Hating to lose him, the systems manager tried this maneuver. He said, "John, we need some one to go out and quiet down these people. Your top assignment is to go out and find out why people don't like this new system. I'm taking you off all other jobs. Find out what they want, then revise the system to give it to them."

The tactic worked. John learned to listen. He exhibited patience others didn't think he possessed. In four months he had revised the system, incorporating most of the requests that the users made. He became the greatest analyst the manager had (the company employed 45). His boss explained:

I was partly to blame for the original mess. I put on an unreasonably tight installation date. John cooperated. He had analytical ability, intelligence, and drive. He designed a good system and put it in within the three months, but nobody would accept it. They continued to use the old system on a manual basis. So it took another four months to do the job over, a total of seven months.

To get people to come along with you does take time. The seven months that the job finally took included constant consultation with the people running the present system. Invariably these individuals make up the same crew that will run any new system. The technical side of the system just mentioned was complete in less than three months. But it was only technically good. People-wise it was a poor system.

The final system overcame the acceptance hurdle and it was technically better as well. The analyst learned much about the systems user's informational needs that he thought had been covered before. He took it for granted that the output of the old system was doing a job.

Getting a system to run on the computer is a technical achievement, but it is not a well-rounded *management systems* achievement. Excellent technical design isn't enough. The system must also run successfully "on people."

Some of the more essential characteristics of a capable analyst include:

1. Analytical ability
2. Mental intelligence (about things)
3. Social intelligence (about people)
4. Technical knowledge (such as how to make a computer do work)
5. The ability to listen
6. A respect for all working functions and the people in the organization
7. A nice balance of patience and drive
8. The ability to communicate both orally and in writing with nonanalysts

Are those desirable characteristics found among women analysts? They are. As a matter of fact, women seem to have more natural social intelligence than do men. Perhaps that is because they've learned how to get along with their fathers, brothers, husbands, and boy friends.

Item 4, technical knowledge, is an essential in this world of computers. But alone it doesn't make anyone a really effective analyst—one who can team up with the people on the working floor to produce a better system.

3. THE TECHNICAL TIDAL WAVE

Analysts, programmers, and the operators of computer systems have had their hands full keeping up with fast-changing techniques. This is one of the reasons they have not been able to concentrate on the problems of communicating with users.

We have moved through three and one-half generations of computers since 1955 . . . and we have moved rapidly from one concept to another. In rapid succession our systems designers have studied integrated systems, automated systems, management information systems, and data base concepts. Along with this we have had frequent changes in the programming languages. Programming itself has become highly complex. A programmer used to write a program to run a job. He still does that, but he must provide, secure, or adapt other types of programs in order to use the computing power of the large computer. The computer hardware requires flexible extensions of its basic design . . . specialized programs called software.

4. THE LANGUAGE BARRIER

To cope with the technical tidal wave, systems analysts have developed a complex language that few laymen understand. This isn't just a language like COBOL, used by programmers to write instructions for the computer.

It is a complex form of shoptalk or jargon. Such a specialized language has been handy, perhaps, in the data processing/systems shop, but it has all but destroyed communication with people outside the shop.

The new, strange words are bad enough; the currently fashionable acronyms are worse:

CPU   central processing unit
DOS   disk operating system
VS   virtual storage
CRT   cathode ray tube
DS   data set
OCR   optical character recognition
I/O   input/output
MICR   magnetic ink character recognition
COM   computer output microfilm

The data processing language is handy in the shop, but the systems user doesn't understand it.

The computer shop language is "greek" to the layman. He isn't likely to know what *virtual storage* means. And certainly the initials VS are even more devoid of meaning to the uninitiated.

The average analyst needs a course on "How to speak to the natives using that old standby of people-to-people communication . . . plain English."

5. TRAINING

The instruction analyst trainees get is at least 80% technical. They learn to write COBOL and to test a program written in it. They learn about the firm's "hardware configurations." Department heads may talk to the group of trainees, to teach them about the business itself.

Some training is given in-house. Much of it comes from the computer manufacturer's training department. Millions of dollars are spent on courses: video-audio programs, seminars, and workshops . . . more millions are spent on magazines, new books, and for information services that update their informational sheets constantly.

Almost all such "systems" training pivots around and assumes the use of the computer.

Indeed, during a discussion of a "pure" system, a young lady analyst asked: "But, Mr. Matthies, I'm confused. How could there possibly be a system without a computer?"

We asked one director of information (he presided over a staff of 275 people) if his analysts didn't also help users develop manual systems out in their departments. He shook his head and said:

Les, we're both old timers at this systems development business. Today the hundreds of manual systems and subsystems get no analytical attention. But even if they had the time, my programmers and analysts wouldn't know how to approach the problem of improving a manual system. They cut their teeth on the computer and that's all they know. At least they're good at what they do know.

I liked that systems manager's remark—"they're good at what they know." They are. Any time you have contact with such systems designers, programmers, or analysts, you'll have to respect their accomplishments. They are a dedicated, sincere, and hard-working group of professionals.

6. LEADERSHIP OPPORTUNITY

Is the systems analyst limited to his technical design skills? Could he (or she) also be a leader/manager? The analyst who develops *great* systems for his organization excels at *both* technical knowledge and "working floor" knowledge. Such a top-level analyst demonstrates both regular intelligence and social intelligence. It takes both.

Leadership in systems design work isn't all that tough. Time after time, analysts who didn't know they had any leadership ability found that they did. They made that discovery when they enlisted the users to help them, forming a systems improvement team.

They let the people (users) in on the creative work from start to finish . . . in the study, analysis, design and installation phases.

Try it yourself. Of course, you must steer the project. But let the people who use (or work in) the system give you a hand. They'll love you for it. They'll accept that new system; even accept it eagerly.

7. WHO ARE SYSTEMS USERS?

The communication gap between systems designers and systems users isn't one-sided. The user often abdicates his responsibility for improving a system in which his people play a role. He feels that the analyst should do all the systems work. He may say: "That's his job. I have other problems."

Users are all the people who do not work in the systems design or in the data processing area. But they use the information provided by the system to help in carrying on their work. Most systems users don't recognize themselves by the title "users." Perhaps "systems owners" better describes their roles.

Users include members of the management team from top to bottom . . . supervisors, foremen, superintendents, controllers, engineering chiefs, purchasing agents. Users also include many of the key workers. The user may be the order processing clerk or that clerk out in shipping who knows her part of the business as well as her boss.

Users include accountants, salesmen, clerks, secretaries, auditors, procedure writers, credit men, order processors, inspectors, statisticians, production people, engineers, and truck drivers.

A user is anyone who puts information into the system or receives information out of the system's files.

When an analyst solicits ideas from the systems user, he exercises a degree of leadership.

8. THE FEAR OF A LITTLE KNOWLEDGE

Many a user has gone through a course in programming . . . gaining knowledge that he has never used. Our controller of a large bakery went all the way . . . learned data processing and computing from the ground up. But being a controller is a demanding, full-time job on its own, and he should not have burdened himself with details of a technology outside his specialty.

It has been the experience of some senior analysts that a "little knowledge" (in the possession of a user) is a dangerous thing.

Of course it is—if the user tries to tell the analyst or the programmer how to run the system on the computer, or if he sets impossible deadlines for the completion of a project. As someone said years ago, "One of the most horrible of sights is to behold ignorance in action."

So analysts have had some unhappy experiences with users who try to tell them what to do. Naturally they are fearful of a user with a little systems knowledge. "He is nothing but trouble," one man said.

But that problem can be overcome by some down-to-earth training for users. A user who understands what a system is, what it can do and what it can't do, is a person who can play an intelligent role on a systems improvement team.

9. WHAT SHOULD THE USER KNOW?

We need to find out what the user should know because we are not going to get many great systems until systems users and systems designers can work effectively as a systems improvement team.

Has there ever really been such cooperation? Yes, in a number or organizations.

What a refreshing experience it is to observe an organization that is using a series of great systems! In one such merchandising organization using computer and terminal equipment, each major system is one that everyone helped to design. Managers, analysts, and workers know those systems, accept them, and use them to the fullest.

The systems/data processing manager is on the company's executive committee. Key employees constantly make suggestions on how to improve certain elements of the system, because everyone can read a grid chart or write a Playscript procedure. The systems are not sophisticated. They are simple, basic, and flexible. Tough transactions are identified and are not handled on a routine (systems) basis. Someone handles them personally. The people do the brain-work; the computer does the mule work.

The company is both prosperous and profitable. All aspects are systematized: sales, inventory, advertising, accounting, order processing, manufacturing, quality control, buying, and shipping. Sales have climbed 300% in the last seven years.

Every user needs to understand what a system is and what it is not. He can't go on thinking of "magic boxes." (One supervisor asked an analyst to provide a report using information that wasn't even in that computer's file.)

One of the key means of bridging the present gap between systems designers and systems users is "know your role." An analyst is a catalyst. He helps to bring into one plan of action (a system) the often divergent views of the men and women who use that system. The user is a contributor of pertinent knowl-edge.

There's another very important reason for opening the user's eyes. With some reasonable amount of education on management systems and some expe-rience gained from rubbing elbows with a professional analyst, the user can do something that needs doing:

★ Show his own staff people how to use the basics of good systems design to improve the subsystems and manual systems that today are getting no attention from professional systems staffs.

There are thousands of subsystems in organizations that operate on a natural basis. The people on the working floor just figure out some way in which they can cooperate . . . and that's all the system does. It works. But not well. It is clumsy, slow, costly, and rife with duplication. The forms are a headache to fill out and are hard to read. They make up that universal headache people call "that blasted paperwork."

Such manual systems can be vastly improved with little effort . . . if the supervisor and his key subordinates acquire just a little training in systems anal-ysis and design.

If they gain a knowledge of only three techniques, users could improve their manual systems substantially. The three techniques are

1. Making a grid chart of the system
2. Writing a Playscript procedure
3. Designing an action form

To get better major systems, top management could hurry along the process of analyst-user cooperation by issuing a policy statement such as this:

Each manager and each supervisor will report annually to the executive committee on at least one major improvement in the systems he or his people use. These improvements shall be provable and will be subject to audit.

To assist line managers, the staff of the systems department will be available to serve as systems and methods consultants.

You may ask: "Will that work?" Yes, it will. It has.

INDEX